MOVE IT!
STUDENTS' BOOK

W0007307

CAROLYN BARRACLOUGH AND KATHERINE STANNETT

SERIES CONSULTANT: CARA NORRIS-RAMIREZ

2 Contents

Starter Unit

Vocabulary

• Countries and nationalities

1 Match the countries (1–8) to the nationalities (a–h).

Country	Nationality
1 Spain	a Greek
2 England	b Mexican
3 Brazil	c French
4 France	d Portuguese
5 Italy	e English
6 Portugal	f Spanish
7 Mexico	g Brazilian
8 Greece	h Italian

2 Match the countries from Exercise 1 to the letters (a–h) on the map. Do you know any other countries?

a *England*

• Numbers

3 Add/Subtract the numbers. Write the answer.

1 fifteen + twenty-six *forty-one*
2 one hundred twelve – nineteen
3 eighty-five + seventy-nine
4 one thousand six – eleven
5 sixty-one + six hundred two

```
  15
+ 26
----
  41
```

4 Listen. Write the numbers you hear in your notebook.
1.2

• Spelling

5 Say the letters to spell these words.
1.3 Listen and check.

1 B-R-A-Z-I-L-I-A-N
2 E-L-E-V-E-N
3 B-A-C-K-P-A-C-K
4 M-P-3 P-L-A-Y-E-R
5 S-E-C-O-N-D-A-R-Y

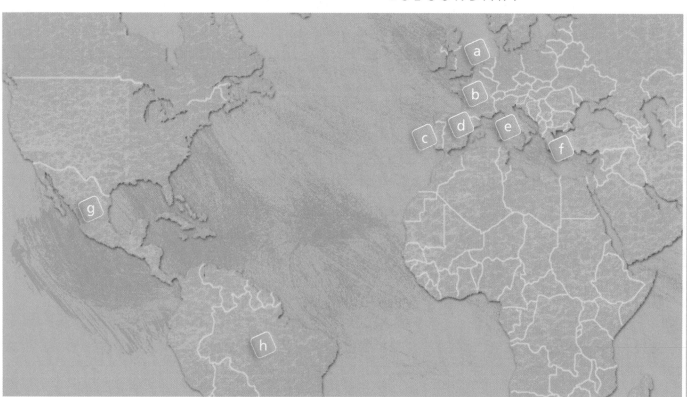

Classroom objects

6 Look for one minute. Remember and write the objects in your notebook.

1 *interactive whiteboard*

Days of the week and months of the year

7 Put the days in the correct order. Which day is your favorite?

- Wednesday
- Saturday
- Friday
- Sunday
- Monday *1*
- Tuesday
- Thursday

8 Find four months in each line.

1 cow*november*armarchapplejanuarybreaddecember
2 daycookjuneolyaprilgremondayoctoberpenciljuly
3 februarygreenmayaugustairportcarseptember

Classroom language

9 Match the sentences to the speaker. Is it a student (S) or a teacher (T)? Listen and repeat.

1.4

1 Open your books! *T*
2 Can you repeat … , please?
3 How do you spell … ?
4 Listen carefully.
5 I'm sorry, I don't understand.
6 Please be quiet!
7 Check your answers.
8 How do you say … in English?
9 What's the homework?

Grammar • To be

1 Study the grammar table.

Affirmative	Negative
I'm (am)	I'm not
You're (are)	You aren't (are not)
He's (is)	He isn't (is not)
She's (is)	She isn't (is not)
It's (is)	It isn't (is not)
We're (are)	We aren't (are not)
They're (are)	They aren't (are not)
Questions and short answers	
Am I ... ?	Yes, I am. / No, I'm not.
Is he/she/it ... ?	Yes, he/she/it is. No, he/she/it isn't.
Are you/we/they ... ?	Yes, you/we/they are. No, you/we/they aren't.

Watch Out!
Subject pronouns
- I
- You
- He
- She
- It
- We
- They

2 Choose the correct options.

1 My friend Leo *is* / *are* American.
2 We *aren't* / *isn't* from London. We are Spanish.
3 I *are* / *am* in a new class.
4 *Is* / *Are* they at the park?
5 You *is* / *are* in the classroom!

3 Complete the sentences.

1 He *is* a boy but she .... a boy; she .... a girl!
2 .... he a doctor?
3 I .... French, I'm Italian. I come from Milan.
4 .... you twelve years old? You are very tall!
5 .... it a cat? No, I think it's a dog.
6 You .... in English class with Ms. Taylor.

• *Wh* questions

4 Study the grammar table.

Wh questions
What's your name?
Where are you from?
How old are you?
When is your birthday?
Why are you happy?
Who is your sister?

5 Complete the questions.

1 *Where* is Paris?
   It's in France. Paris is the capital of France.
2 .... is your brother?
   He's fifteen. And my little sister is two.
3 .... is that?
   It's a bicycle.
4 .... are you happy?
   I am happy because it's my birthday today.
5 .... is your best friend?
   My best friend is Pedro.
6 .... is Halloween?
   It's in October.

6 Make questions.

1 name / What's / your ?
   What's your name?
2 you / from / Where / are ?
3 How / are / you / old ?
4 is / your / birthday / When ?
5 you / happy / Why / are ?
6 Who / best friend / your / is ?

7 In pairs, ask and answer the questions in Exercise 6.

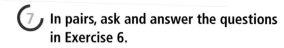

• This/That/These/Those

Singular		Plural	
This is a pen.	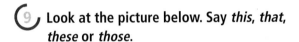	These are erasers.	
That is a desk.		Those are chairs.	

9 Look at the picture below. Say *this, that, these* or *those*.

1 *That* is an interactive whiteboard.
2 .... are backpacks.
3 .... are chairs.
4 .... are pens.
5 .... is a pencil.
6 .... are erasers.
7 .... are rulers.
8 .... is a calculator.

Watch Out!
This is a pen. NOT ~~This is pen.~~
These are chairs. NOT ~~These are a chairs.~~

Reading

1 **Look at the text. How many people are in the Wildlife Club?**

Welcome to ...

The Wildlife Club!

- The Wildlife Club ... **what** is it?
  It's a great nature club at our school.
- The Wildlife Club ... **when** is it?
  It's on Thursday afternoons, from 3:30 to 4:30.
- The Wildlife Club ... **who** is in it?
  Say hello to our Wildlife Club members!

I'm Nick. I'm in 8th grade, and I'm 13 years old. My favorite animal is my dog, Sunny. The Wildlife Club is cool! Wildlife and nature are very important to me.

I'm Julia, and this is my brother, Leo. I'm 12, and Leo is 8. He is in the Wildlife Club because animals and nature are his favorite things.

2 **Read the text again. Are the statements true (T) or false (F)?**

1.5

1 The Wildlife Club is an arts club. *F*
2 The Wildlife Club is on Friday afternoons.
3 Nick is 13 years old.
4 Sunny is a rabbit.
5 Leo and Julia are friends.

Listening and Speaking

3 Look at the photo. Find the new member of the Wildlife Club.

4 1.6 Listen to the conversation. Who is the new member?

5 1.6 Listen to the conversation again and complete the form.

Wildlife Club
New Member Form

Name *Monica*

Age ....

Grade ....

What's your favorite animal?

....

6 1.6 Listen to the conversation again. Are these statements true (T) or false (F)?

1 Monica is in 7th grade.
2 Nick is in 7th grade.
3 Sunny is in the Wildlife Club.

7 In pairs, ask and answer to complete your profile.

Wildlife Club
New Member Form

Name ....

Age ....

Grade ....

What's your favorite animal?

....

✓ **My assessment profile:** Workbook page 126

Grammar
Have; Possessive adjectives;
Possessive *'s*

Vocabulary
Objects; Adjectives

■ Speaking
■ Talking about position
■ Writing
A personal profile

Word list page 43
Workbook page 104

Vocabulary • Objects

1 Match the photos to these words. Then listen, check and repeat.

1.7

camera
cell phone
comics   *1*
DVD
game console
guitar
ice skates
laptop
magazine
MP3 player
poster
skateboard
wallet
watch

2 Match the definitions to seven objects from Exercise 1.

1 It's a musical instrument. *guitar*
2 It's a movie.
3 It's a computer.
4 It's a small clock.
5 They're stories with superheroes.
6 It's a board with wheels.
7 It's a big picture.

3 Listen and find the missing letter.

1.8   1 wallet /   3 camera
       2 comics   4 skateboard

4 Think of three words with missing letters. In pairs, ask and answer.

What letter is missing?
W - A - C - H.

It's T.

Good.

Brain Trainer
Activity 3
Go to page 112

Reading

1 Look at the photos. Who has these things: Lisa (L) or Emilio (E)?

1 a skateboard
2 a camera
3 comics
4 posters

2 Read and check your answers to Exercise 1.

3 Read the text. How many objects do Lisa and
1.9 Emilio mention?

4 Read the text again. Answer the questions.
1.9
1 Where is Lisa from? *She's from Canada.*
2 Where is Emilio from?
3 What is Lisa a fan of?
4 What is Emilio a fan of?
5 Name *The Simpsons* objects.
6 Name the soccer objects.

5 What about you? In pairs, ask and answer.
1 What TV show/team/sport are you a fan of?
2 Who is your favorite TV character/athlete?

I'm a fan of *Glee.*

I'm a New York Yankees fan.

Fans of the Month

Simpsons fan!

My brother and I are *Simpsons* fans. We have about two hundred comics, and they have very funny stories and pictures. Do you have a *Simpsons* comic?

The Simpsons computer game is cool, but we don't have a *Simpsons* DVD. I have a *Simpsons* watch and a big skateboard with Bart Simpson on it. My brother doesn't have a skateboard, but he has a guitar with a picture of Homer on it. It's awesome!

Oh, and guess what? My name is Lisa ... but my brother's name isn't Bart!

Lisa, Canada

Soccer fan!

I'm from Mar del Plata in Argentina. We have a great soccer team here. I have a soccer shirt, a scarf, a wallet and a backpack ... and a lot of posters on my bedroom walls! Mom and Dad are big soccer fans, too. Dad has a blue laptop, a blue cell phone and a blue car!

I also have photos of some players on my camera. Messi is my favorite player. He is an excellent goal scorer!

Emilio, Argentina

Grammar • Have

Affirmative		
I/You/We/They	have	a new DVD.
He/She/It	has	

Negative		
I/You/We/They	don't have (do not have)	a new DVD.
He/She/It	doesn't have (does not have)	

Questions		
Do I/you/we/they	have	a new DVD?
Does he/she/it	have	

Short answers
Yes, I/you/we/they do. / No, I/you/we/they don't.
Yes, he/she/it does. / No, he/she/it doesn't.

Grammar reference Workbook page 86

Watch Out!
do not → don't
does not → doesn't

1 Study the grammar table. Complete the rules.

1 We say I / .... / .... / .... have or *don't have*.
2 We say he / .... / .... has or *doesn't have*.
3 The question form of *they have* is .... ?
4 The short form of *do not have* is .... .
5 The short form of *does not have* is .... .

2 Choose the correct options.

1 Carla and Luisa *has / have* posters of Lady Gaga.
2 Elena *doesn't have / don't have* a *Twilight* DVD.
3 *Do / Does* your parents have a laptop?
4 I *has / have* a camera in my backpack.
5 Harry *doesn't have / don't have* a Superman comic.
6 *Do / Does* Angela have a new watch?

3 Find the subject + verb. Write the full form in your notebook.

1 He doesn't have a new game console.
   He does not have
2 They don't have a laptop.
3 We don't have posters for the classroom.
4 The teacher doesn't have an MP3 player.

4 Complete the text with *have* or *has*.

My dad is a DJ. He ¹ *has* a radio show. He gets famous people on his show. He ² .... a lot of autographs from the famous people. He ³ .... autographs from Will Smith and Angelina Jolie. But he doesn't ⁴ .... an autograph from a sports player. My favorite singer is Katy Perry, but I don't ⁵ .... her autograph. Do you ⁶ .... an autograph from a famous person?

Pronunciation Short forms

5a Look at the verbs. Find the short forms
1.10 and listen.

1 I don't have a cell phone.
2 She doesn't have a magazine.
3 They don't have my ice skates.

b Listen again and repeat.
1.10

6 What about you? In pairs, ask and answer about these objects.

DVD	guitar	magazine
MP3 player	skateboard	watch

Do you have an MP3 player?

Yes, I do.

Vocabulary • Adjectives

1 Match the adjectives (1–7) to the opposite adjectives (a–g).
1.11 Then listen, check and repeat.

1 bad
2 cheap
3 difficult
4 popular
5 boring
6 new
7 small

a expensive
b unpopular
c interesting
d good
e big
f easy
g old

Word list page 43 **Workbook** page 104

2 Choose the correct options. Then listen, check and repeat.

1.12 1 Help! I have this game. It's really *easy / difficult*.

2 We have a sports game for your console. It's from 2007, so it's *new / old*.

3 I have two Rihanna posters. She's great—she's very *popular / unpopular*.

4 Look at this camera. It's $750, so it's *cheap / expensive*.

5 I have about fifteen schoolbooks! I have a *big / small* backpack.

6 I have these cool DVDs. They're very *good / bad*.

7 Do you have *New Moon*? It's an *interesting / boring* novel. Read it now!

3 Listen and guess the adjective.
1.13 More than one answer may be possible.

> Well done! Excellent work!

> Is it "good"?

4 Complete the sentences with adjectives from Exercise 1.

1 The movie *The Pirates of the Caribbean* is *good*.
2 A Ferrari is ... .
3 Keira Knightley is ... .
4 The Harry Potter books are ... .
5 Brazil is ... .
6 I think English is ... .
7 Usher's songs are ... .

5 Choose one thing from each group. Use an adjective and write a sentence in your notebook.

• computer game / book / movie / song
• sports star / actor / singer
• object in your school / home

The computer game is difficult.

6 Look at the objects in Exercise 2. In pairs, ask and answer.

> Is the camera expensive?

> Yes, it is.

Brain Trainer Activity 4
Go to page 112

Speaking and Listening

1 **Look at the photo and answer the questions.**

1 Who is in Nick's room?
2 Name three objects in Nick's room.

2 **Listen and read the conversation.**
1.14 **Answer the questions.**

1 Is Nick's room big or small? *It's small.*
2 Does Nick have a game console?
3 Does Nick have a soccer game?
4 Are Nick's ice skates on the bed?
5 What is under the desk?

3 **Act out the conversation in groups of three.**

Julia	This is a nice room!
Nick	Thanks. It's small, but it's OK.
Julia	Oh look, Sunny's in your room.
Nick	Sit, Sunny. Good dog.
Leo	Is this your game console, Nick?
Nick	Yes, it is.
Leo	Cool! What games do you have?
Nick	I have a new soccer game—it's really difficult!
Leo	Where is it?
Nick	It's next to the game console.
Oh, my ice skates are on the desk! Sorry.
Leo	Hey, Nick, what's that under the desk?
Nick	Oh, it's my skateboard.
Leo	Great. I have one, too.

Say it in your language ...
Cool!
Great.

4 Look back at the conversation. Who says what?

1 It's next to the game console. *Nick*
2 Sunny's in your room.
3 What's that under the desk?
4 My ice skates are on the desk!

5 Read the phrases for talking about position.

Talking about position
Sunny's in your room.
Where is it?
It's next to the game console.
My ice skates are on the desk!
What's that under the desk?

6 Match the pictures to these words.

| behind   in   in front of   next to   on   under |

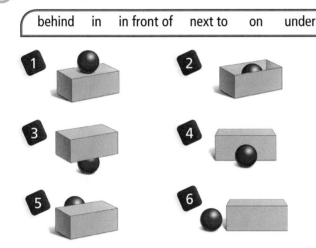

7 Listen to the conversation. Act out
1.15 the conversation in pairs.

Ryan Where's the ¹ magazine?
Tania Is it ² on the desk?
Ryan No.
Tania Look. It's ³ under the desk.

8 Work in pairs. Replace the words in purple in Exercise 7. Use these words and/or your own ideas. Act out the conversation.

> Where's the laptop?

> Is it next to the desk?

1 DVD / game console / cell phone

2 behind / next to / under

3 in front of / on

Grammar • Possessive adjectives and Possessive 's

Possessive adjectives		Possessive 's
I	my	**One person**
you	your	Monica's bag.
he	his	Nick's dog.
she	her	
it	its	**Two or more people**
we	our	My parents' car.
they	their	John and Tom's room.

Grammar reference Workbook page 86

1 Study the grammar table and learn.

2 Make sentences. Change the underlined words.

1 It's <u>Julia's</u> watch.
  It's her watch.
2 That's <u>my parents'</u> room.
3 Those are <u>my brother's and my</u> DVDs.
4 It's <u>Mr. Green's</u> laptop.
5 Are these <u>Anna's</u> books?
6 This is <u>the boy's</u> ball.

3 Copy the sentences. Put the apostrophe in the correct place.

1 I have my moms wallet.
  I have my mom's wallet.
2 Do you have Andys cell phone?
3 Here is my grandparents house.
4 This is the teachers MP3 player.
5 Where is Marinas dads camera?
6 My sisters names are Olivia and Lina.

4 What about you? In pairs, ask and answer questions about five objects in the classroom.

> Is this your pen?

> No, it's Rafa's pen.

Reading

1 Look quickly at the text and the photos. Answer the questions.

1 What type of text is it?
 a a quiz
 b a competition
 c an interview
2 Who are the characters in the photo?
 a They're from a movie.
 b They're from a book.
 c They're from a play.

My dad in his *Star Wars* costume.

Help!

Dad Has an Embarrassing Hobby!

This week's problem page interview is with Nicole from Montreal, Canada.

■ **Do you have a special collection, Nicole?**

No, I don't have a collection, but my dad has a *Star Wars* collection. It's his favorite movie, but it's an old movie now, and I'm not a big *Star Wars* fan. Here's a photo of Dad with his friends at a *Star Wars* convention. Just look at their costumes—it's really embarrassing!

■ **Is it a big collection?**

Yes, it is. Dad has hundreds of props and costumes from the *Star Wars* movies. He has DVDs and posters in the living room. He has Luke Skywalker's *lightsaber* in the dining room, and *Star Wars* books and magazines in his bedroom, too. I have a *Star Wars* bed in my room with Darth Vader on it. Yuck! Our house is full!

■ **Is this a problem?**

Well, it's OK because we have a big shed in the backyard, but guess what? That's full of *Star Wars* things, too. Dad is happy with his collection, but Mom isn't happy because *Star Wars* things are very expensive.

My dad's collection.

Key Words		
embarrassing	convention	costumes
props	shed	

2 Read and check your answers to Exercise 1.

3 Read the interview again. Are the statements
1.16 true (T) or false (F)?

1 Nicole is a fan of *Star Wars* movies. *F*
2 Nicole's dad has a *Stars Wars* costume.
3 Her dad has thousands of *Star Wars* things.
4 Nicole has a *Star Wars* bed.
5 Her parents have a small shed in the backyard.
6 *Star Wars* things aren't cheap.

Listening

1 Listen to three interviews. Match the speaker
1.17 to the interview.

 Interview 1   a Peter's mom
 Interview 2   b Peter's brother
 Interview 3   c Peter

2 Listen again. Answer the questions.
1.17 1 Who has a *Karate Kid* collection?
  a Peter's brother b Peter's mom c Peter
 2 What is Peter's mom's opinion?
  a The collection is big.
  b The collection is small.
  c The collection is cheap.
 3 What is Peter's brother's opinion of *The Karate Kid*?
  a It's cool. b It's great. c It's boring.

Writing • A personal profile

1 Read the Writing File.

Writing File   Punctuation 1

We use punctuation to make our writing clear.

- **We use capital letters (*A*, *B*, *C* ...) for the names of people, places, songs, games and groups.**

- **We also use capital letters for the first person *I*.**

- **We use periods (.) at the end of sentences.**

- **Apostrophes (') can show missing letters—for example, in short forms.**

- **Apostrophes can also show possession.**

---

2 Read the profile. Match the words in blue to the rules in the Writing File.

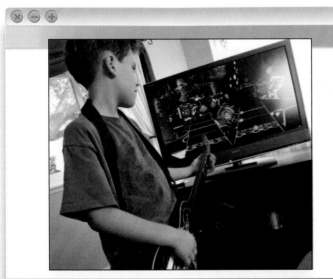

My favorite things

My name's ¹ **Billy**, and ² **I'm** eleven years old. I'm from ³ **Chicago**. It's a big city in ⁴ **Illinois**. My favorite thing is my new game console. I ⁵ **don't** have a lot of games because ⁶ **they're** expensive. I have about five. My favorite is ⁷ *Guitar Hero* because I have an electric guitar for this game. ⁸ **It's** a great game, and the ⁹ **game's** songs are good. My favorite song is ¹⁰ *Ruby* by ¹¹ **Kaiser Chiefs**.

3 Rewrite the sentences. Use capital letters, periods and apostrophes.

1 his names luke   *His name's Luke.*
2 shes my sister
3 im thirteen years old
4 our teachers name is john day
5 they dont have a game console

4 Read the profile again. Answer the questions.

1 How old is Billy?   *He's eleven years old.*
2 Where is he from?
3 What are his two favorite things?
4 Why doesn't he have a lot of games?
5 Why is *Guitar Hero* his favorite game?
6 What is his favorite song?

5 Answer the questions.

1 What's your name, and how old are you?
2 Where are you from?
3 What are your favorite things?
4 Give extra information about your favorite things.

6 Write a description of you and your favorite things. Use "My favorite things" and your answers from Exercise 5.

My favorite things   ⊗

Paragraph 1
- Your personal information
  My name is ... , and I'm ... . (age)
  I'm from ... .

Paragraph 2
- Your favorite things
  My favorite thing is ... / My favorite things are ... and ... .
- Extra information
  I have ... . (number)
  I don't have ... .
  My favorite ... is ... because ... .

Remember!
- Use capital letters, apostrophes and periods in the correct places.
- Use the vocabulary in this unit.
- Check your grammar and spelling.

Refresh Your Memory!

Grammar • Review

1 Make affirmative and negative sentences with *have*.

	Felipe	Adriana and Damon
1 a guitar	✓	✗
2 a skateboard	✗	✓
3 a game console	✗	✗
4 an MP3 player	✓	✓

1 *Felipe has a guitar.*

2 Make questions and short answers about the things in Exercise 1.

1 *Does Felipe have a guitar? Yes, he does.*

3 Complete the sentences with the correct possessive adjective.

1 I have *my* lunch in this bag.
2 Do you have .... MP3 player?
3 Mr. Smith has .... watch.
4 Mrs. Jones doesn't have .... laptop.
5 We have .... magazines.
6 They have .... cameras.

4 Rewrite the sentences. Use possessive *'s or s'*.

1 Kayla / laptop / is new
  Kayla's laptop is new.
2 My brother / camera / is expensive
3 Jessica and Oscar / dog / is small
4 My teacher / book / is interesting
5 Fabio / favorite soccer player / is Ronaldo
6 My cousins / DVD / is old

Vocabulary • Review

5 Complete the sentences with these words.

cell phone	comics	laptops
MP3 player	skateboard	watch

1 The teacher doesn't have any *comics* in her classroom.
2 My .... is in my bag.
3 I have some new songs on my .... .
4 I don't have a .... , but I have a bike.
5 What time is it? I don't have my .... .
6 The school has .... for students.

6 Find seven adjectives.

from	**small**	the	**get**	**unpopular**
fan	name	**easy**	**cheap**	**look**
expensive	**room**	**bad**	**boring**	

Speaking • Review

7 Look at the picture and complete the conversation.
1.18 Then listen and check.

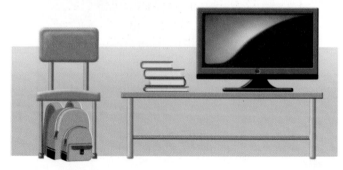

A Where's my backpack?
B It's there, ¹ .... the chair.
A Are my schoolbooks ² .... my bag?
B No, they aren't.
A Where are they?
B They're ³ .... the table, ⁴ .... the TV—here!

Dictation

8 Listen and write in your notebook.
1.19

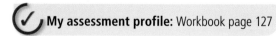

✓ **My assessment profile:** Workbook page 127

20th-Century Painting

On this page are examples of two different styles of early-20th-century painting: Cubism and Pointillism. One painting is a still life—a painting of objects such as vases, bowls or mugs. The other painting is a landscape—this is a painting of the countryside.

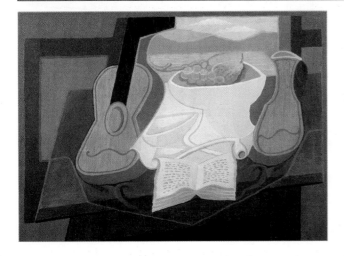

Guitar and Fruit Bowl

This picture has a guitar, a fruit bowl, a bottle and a book in it. Juan Gris's style of painting is Cubism. The picture has a lot of geometrical shapes, and the colors are not very bright. This is typical of Cubist paintings. Other famous Cubist artists are Pablo Picasso and Georges Braque.

Washing in the Sun

This painting is from 1905. There is a basket with some laundry in it. The trees are blue, and there are long shadows. Pellizza da Volpedo's style of painting is called Pointillism. Pointillist paintings have very small dots of color. Georges Seurat and Paul Signac are other famous Pointillist artists.

Reading

1 **Match the artists to the pictures.**
   1 Pellizza da Volpedo
   2 Juan Gris

2 **Read about the two paintings.**
1.20 **Answer the questions.**
   1 Which two styles of painting can you see on this page?
   2 Name three Cubist artists.
   3 Which of these paintings is a landscape? Which is a still life?
   4 Which style of painting uses bright colors?

My Art File

3 **In pairs, find out about another famous 20th-century painting. Think about:**
   • the artist
   • the style of painting
   • other artists in the same style
   • the objects/people in the painting
   • why you like it

4 **Design a poster about your painting. Use your notes from Exercise 3 to help you. Then present your poster to your class.**

Grammar
There is/There are;
Some/Any; Can/Can't
for ability

Vocabulary
■ Places in a town;
■ Action verbs

■ **Speaking**
Orders and warnings

Writing
A description of a town

Word list page 43
Workbook page 105

Vocabulary • Places in a town

1 Match the places in the picture to these words. Then listen, check and repeat.
1.21

bank
bus station
café
hospital *1*
library
movie theater
museum
park
police station
post office
shopping mall
sports complex
town square
train station

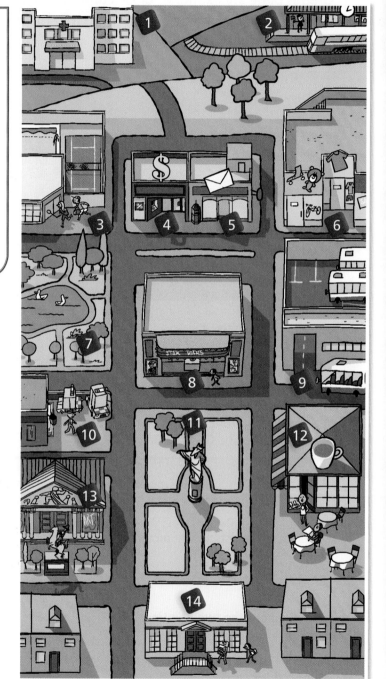

2 Where can you find these things? Match the things to the places in Exercise 1.

1 ticket *movie theater*
2 book
3 ball
4 tree
5 money
6 coffee

3 Read the clues and find the places in the picture.

1 It's behind the shopping mall.
   train station
2 It's behind the park.
3 It's next to the post office.
4 It's in front of the movie theater.
5 It's next to the shopping mall.
6 It's in front of the police station.

4 In pairs, make a list of other places in a town.

supermarket, playground

Brain Trainer
Activity 3
Go to page 113

Reading

1 Look at the text. What do you think it is about?
  a parks
  b virtual towns
  c shopping malls

2 Read the text and check your answer to Exercise 1.

3 Read the text again. Are the statements true (T) or false (F)?
1.22
  1 TanyaCity doesn't have any museums. *F*
  2 TanyaCity has a library.
  3 Fabville doesn't have any houses.
  4 Fabville has a school.
  5 Garboton has some stores.
  6 Garboton has a train station.

4 What about you? Invent your Cybertown. In pairs, ask and answer.
  1 What's the name of the town?
  2 Where is it?
  3 What places does it have? Where are they?

> What's the name of the town?

> It's MusicTown.

Cybertown
It's Our Town, It's Your Town

Tanya
My Cybertown is TanyaCity. I have a big house and a lot of friends. There are two shopping malls next to my house, with a lot of great stores. There's a museum and a park in front of the library, and there are some big houses behind my school. TanyaCity is a beautiful town.

Ben
My Cybertown is Fabville. It's really cool. I ♥ sports, and Fabville has a sports complex and three parks. My house is next to a big library. In the town square, there is a bank and a small post office, and there's a very big hospital. Next to the hospital there's a great café. In Fabville there aren't any schools!

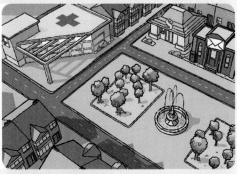

Sanjay
Garboton is my Cybertown. It has very good connections—there's a train station and a bus station. There's a town square in Garboton, and there are some stores, but there isn't a shopping mall. There isn't a museum or a library, but there's a big police station. It's my police station! I'm the Chief of Police in Garboton!

Grammar • There is/There are; Some/Any

Affirmative
There's (There is) a museum.
There are some houses/two shopping malls.

Negative
There isn't (is not) a library.
There aren't (are not) any schools.

Questions and short answers	
Is there a hospital?	Yes, there is. No, there isn't.
Are there any houses?	Yes, there are. No, there aren't.

Grammar reference Workbook page 88

Watch Out!

There are → some cafés.
There aren't → any restaurants.
Are there → any restaurants?

1 **Study the grammar table. Complete the rules with** *there is, there are, there isn't* **and** *there aren't.*

1 We use .... and .... with singular nouns,
   e.g., *a museum, a cat, a house.*
2 We use .... and .... with plural nouns,
   e.g., *some/any stores, a lot of schools.*

2 **Choose** *There is* **or** *There are* **to complete the sentences.**

1 *There is* a big shopping mall in our town.
2 .... three Canadian girls in my school.
3 .... some books under your bed.
4 .... a big party on Saturday. It's my birthday!
5 .... a new interactive whiteboard
   in my classroom.
6 .... two swimming pools in this sports complex.

3 **Complete the conversation. Then listen and check.**

1.23
Tom What's in your town, Emma?
Emma ¹ *There's* a big movie theater and an
   international school. ² .... any parks.
   ³ .... any parks in your town?
Tom Yes, ⁴ ..... . ⁵ .... some beautiful parks, and
   ⁶ .... a shopping mall called GoShop.
   ⁷ .... a sports complex in your town?
Emma No, ⁸ ..... . But ⁹ .... a modern art museum.

4 **Make questions and answers.**

1 any good movies / on TV? (✗)
   Are there any good movies on TV?
   No, there aren't.
2 a cell phone / in your bag? (✓)
3 a swimming pool / in your house? (✗)
4 any American students / in your class? (✓)
5 any libraries / in your town? (✗)

5 **Look at the information about Sandra's backpack. Find and correct five mistakes in the text.**

There isn't a wallet.

My backpack

pen	✓
wallet	✗
DVDs	✗
apple	✗
MP3 player	✗
laptop	✓
books	✗
magazine	✓

There's a pen in my backpack, and there's a wallet. There are some DVDs, and there's an apple and an MP3 player. There isn't a laptop. There aren't any books in my backpack, but there's a magazine.

6 **What about you? Imagine you have a new backpack. What do you have in it? Write six sentences.**

In my backpack, there's ... .

Vocabulary • Action verbs

1 Match the pictures to these words. Then listen, check and repeat.
1.24

bike	climb *1*	dance	fly	juggle	jump
play	run	sing	skate	swim	walk

Word list page 43   **Workbook** page 105

2 Match the verbs (1–8) to the phrases (a–h).

1 play *d*
2 swim
3 juggle
4 climb
5 jump
6 bike
7 sing
8 run

a six balls
b a song
c a tree, a mountain
d a game, soccer, the guitar
e to school
f 100 meters, in the pool
g very high
h a marathon

3 Make complete sentences with the information in Exercise 2.

1 *I play soccer.*

Pronunciation
Silent letters

4a Listen and find the silent letter in each word.
1.25

1 walk
2 climb
3 guitar
4 talk
5 know

b Listen again and repeat.
1.25

**Brain Trainer
Activity 4**
Go to page 113

Chatroom Orders and warnings

Speaking and Listening

1 Look at the photo. Are these things in the photo?

1 backpack ✓ 5 dog 8 laptop
2 book 6 food 9 map
3 canoes 7 ice skates 10 wallet
4 cell phone

2 Listen and read the conversation.
1.26 Are the statements true (T) or false (F)?

1 There is a lake in the park. *T*
2 The park isn't a good place for a picnic.
3 Monica has the map.
4 The food is in Nick's bag.
5 Leo is very careful.
6 Julia isn't very happy.
7 At the end, their lunch is in the lake.

3 Act out the conversation in groups of four.

Monica	Where are we now? Look at the map, Nick.
Nick	OK, we're at the lake. The park's a really good place for our picnic.
Leo	A picnic! Great! Oh, and our lunch is in my backpack. Apples! Watch me! I can juggle!
Julia	Leo, be careful!
Monica	Leo! Don't play with our food!
Nick	Come on, everyone. Let's go!
Leo	Hang on, guys. Wait for us!
Julia	Don't shout, Leo!
Leo	OK. Look! I can dance in the canoe.
Julia	Leo! Please, don't do that. Stop!
Leo	Oh no! Help!
Monica	Are you OK, Leo? Can you swim?
Leo	Yes, I can, but there's a small problem.
Nick	What?
Leo	Our lunch is in the lake.
M, N & J	Oh Leo!

Say it in your language ...

Let's go!
Hang on.

4 Look back at the conversation. Complete the instructions.

1 W a t c h me!
2 B_ careful!
3 Don't p _ _ _ with our food!
4 W _ _ _ for us!
5 Don't s _ _ _ _!
6 S _ _ p!

5 Read the phrases for giving orders and warnings.

Orders

Watch me!
Don't play … !
Wait for us!
Don't shout!
Please, don't do that.

Warnings

Be careful!
Stop!
Help!

6 Listen to the conversations. Act out the conversations in pairs.
1.27

Julia	Leo, don't play with [1] our food.
Leo	OK, Julia. But don't shout!
Julia	Leo, don't [2] swim in the lake.
Leo	OK, Julia. But don't shout!

7 Work in pairs. Replace the words in purple in Exercise 6 with these words. Act out the conversations.

Leo, don't play with my camera.

OK, Julia. But don't shout!

1 my cell phone / my laptop / my book

2 run / climb trees / dance in the canoe

8 Act out the conversations again with your own words and ideas.

Grammar • Can/Can't for ability

Affirmative

I/You/He/She/It/We/They can juggle.

Negative

I/You/He/She/It/We/They can't dance.

Questions and short answers

Can I/you/he/she/it/we/they play the guitar?
Yes, I/you/he/she/it/we/they can.
No, I/you/he/she/it/we/they can't.

Grammar reference Workbook page 88

1 Study the grammar table. Choose the correct rule, 1 or 2.

1 We say can/can't + to + verb.
2 We say can/can't + verb.

2 Look at the table. Then read the sentences and say Jon, Dan or Matt.

	sing	dance	juggle
Jon	✓	✗	✗
Dan	✗	✗	✓
Matt	✓	✓	✗
Anna	✗	✓	✓
Meg	✓	✓	✗

1 This boy can sing, and he can dance, but he can't juggle. *Matt*
2 This boy can't dance, and he can't juggle, but he can sing.
3 This boy can juggle, but he can't sing, and he can't dance.

3 Complete the sentences for Anna and Meg.
Anna can … .
Meg can … .

4 Make questions with can.

1 ride a bike? *Can you ride a bike?*
2 juggle?
3 sing?
4 play tennis?
5 play the piano?
6 climb trees?

Reading

1 Look at the photos. What animals can you see?

Great Parks in New York City

► **Central Park**

This is a very big park in the middle of Manhattan in New York City—it's 3.4 square kilometers. You can walk around the park and look at the trees, plants and lakes. You can watch the beautiful ducks in the lakes. You can also see a lot of fountains in this park. There are over 40 fountains here! You can bring your bike and ride around the park. There is an amazing view of the park from Belvedere Castle. You can play baseball or have a picnic in the park, or you can go fishing in the lake. You can also get lunch at one of the many food carts in the park. The food is great!

► **Bronx Park**

This famous New York park is the home of the Bronx Zoo and the New York Botanical Garden. You can walk for three kilometers along the Bronx River. There are many species of fish and birds to see here. It's a great experience! You can visit the Bronx Zoo in the southern half of the park to see animals from other parts of the world—for example, flamingos. The park also has playgrounds, basketball courts, and football and soccer fields.

Key Words		
view (n)	castle	to play baseball
to go fishing	species	experience

2 Read the text and check your answer to Exercise 1.

3 Read the text. Answer the questions.

1.28
1 Where is Central Park?
   It is in the middle of Manhattan in New York.
2 What animals can you see in Central Park?
3 What famous building has an amazing view of Central Park?
4 What two places can you find in Bronx Park?
5 How long is the part of the Bronx River in Bronx Park?
6 What animals can you see near the river?

4 Read the text again. Choose *Central Park* (CP)
1.28 or *Bronx Park* (BP).

1 It's in the middle of New York City. *CP*
2 You can see flamingos here.
3 You can have a picnic here.
4 You can walk along a river.
5 You can play soccer.
6 You can ride a bike in this place.

Listening

1 Listen to the audition. Say *Latika, Kate,*
1.29 or *Latika and Kate.*

TALENT WANTED!

Tuesday, November 7
Auditions at the Regal Movie Theater,
3 p.m.

1 She can climb trees.
2 She can swim.
3 She can't sing.
4 She can dance.
5 She can jump up high.
6 She can run really fast.

Writing • A description of a town

1 Read the Writing File.

> **Writing File**   Linking words
>
> - There's a movie theater and a library in my town.
> - There's a swimming pool, but there isn't a sports complex.
> - Jess can't dance, but she can sing.
> - I can't swim or ride a bike.
> - There isn't a shopping mall or a park.

2 Read Emma's description of her hometown. Find examples of *and*, *or* and *but*.

My Hometown

In my hometown, there is a swimming pool, (and) there's a library, but there isn't a sports complex or a museum. There are a lot of houses and stores, but there aren't any movie theaters. There are two restaurants, and there are four cafés. There are some parks, and there's a shopping mall, but there isn't a bus station or a train station. There is a post office, but there isn't a bank. My hometown is small, but it's great.

3 Choose the correct options.

1 I can play soccer, *and / but* I can't play tennis.
2 In Paris there are a lot of restaurants *and / but* cafés.
3 There isn't a police station *but / or* a bank.
4 There aren't any new students at my school, *and / but* there are two new teachers.
5 We can have a picnic *and / but* ride our bikes.

4 Read Emma's description again. What does she have in her hometown?

1 a swimming pool ✓
2 a library
3 a sports complex
4 a museum
5 some houses
6 some stores
7 some parks
8 a shopping mall
9 a bus station
10 a train station
11 a post office

5 Imagine a town or think about your hometown. What is in your town? Take notes. Use the list from Exercise 4.

6 Write a description of your town. Use "My town" and your notes from Exercise 5.

> **My town**   ⊗
>
> 1 Name
> *My town is called ... .*
> 2 Description
> *In ... there is a/are some ... .*
> *In ... there isn't a/aren't any ... .*
> 3 Conclusion
> *My town is ... .*

> **Remember!**
> - Use *and*, *or* and *but*.
> - Use the vocabulary in this unit.
> - Check your grammar, spelling, and punctuation.

Refresh Your Memory!

Grammar • Review

1 **Choose the correct options.**

1 There *is / are* two parks behind my school.
2 There *is / are* a calculator on my desk.
3 There *isn't / aren't* a train station in my town, but there *is / are* a bus station.
4 There *isn't / aren't* any comics in my bag.
5 **A** *Is / Are* there a post office next to the shopping mall?
 B No, there *isn't / aren't*.
6 **A** *Is / Are* there any posters in your classroom?
 B Yes. There *is / are* five posters in our classroom.

2 **Look at the list. Make sentences.**

There is one Spanish student in Class 5b.

International School Class 5b	
Spanish students	1
Greek students	0
French students	5
English students	2
Brazilian students	1
Portuguese students	0
Mexican students	4

3 **Complete the text with *can* or *can't* and the verbs.**

My brother, James, [1] *can climb* (✔ climb), and he [2] .... (✔ juggle), but he [3] .... (✘ run) fast. My sister, Hatty, [4] .... (✔ dance), but she [5] .... (✘ sing). I [6] .... (✘ dance), and I [7] .... (✘ juggle), but I [8] .... (✔ swim).

4 **Make questions and answers.**

1 you / speak English? ✔
 Can you speak English? Yes, I can.
2 your friends / skate? ✘
3 your teacher / swim? ✘
4 Fred / play chess? ✔
5 Fred's dog / dance? ✘
6 your dad / fly a plane? ✘

Vocabulary • Review

5 **Look at the pictures and complete the places.**

1 *library* 2 t .... s .... 3 h .... 4 c ....

5 p .... 6 s .... c .... 7 p .... o .... 8 b .... s ....

6 **Complete the sentences with these verbs.**

bike	sing	juggle	run
~~jump~~	dance	climb	play

1 Trev can *jump* very high.
2 Dave and Sarah can .... beautiful songs.
3 I can't .... the guitar.
4 My dad can .... six balls.
5 I can't .... up that tree!
6 My sister can .... the tango.
7 I can't .... to school because I don't have a bicycle.
8 Can you .... fast?

Speaking • Review

7 **Complete the sentences with these words.**
1.30 **Then listen and check.**

Be	bike	jump	Open	shout	~~swim~~

1 Don't *swim* in the lake!
2 .... quiet!
3 .... your book.
4 Don't .... in the schoolyard.
5 Don't .... on the desks!
6 Don't .... in the library.

Dictation

8 **Listen and write in your notebook.**
1.31

 My assessment profile: Workbook page 128

Fazila Shirindel's Profile

Age	Home country
14 years old	Afghanistan

City
Kabul

Fazila and Skateistan

Fazila is a 14-year-old girl from Qalai Zaman Khan in Kabul, Afghanistan. Her family is very poor, and Fazila's life is difficult, but she is happy because she is a student at a school in Kabul. The school is called "Skateistan," and it's the first skateboarding school in Kabul.

Skateistan has a big indoor skate park and some classrooms with computers. Children can study English, computer science, journalism, art and music there. There's a special "Back to school" program for children who aren't in school. There are separate school days for boys and for girls because, in Afghanistan, girls and boys don't do activities together, and there are also special classes for disabled children.

After the classes, there is a 50-minute skateboarding lesson for all the girls in Fazila's class. Fazila doesn't have a skateboard, but she can borrow one from the school.

Now Fazila is very good at skateboarding, and she is also a teacher at Skateistan. "Life is hard for me because my family is poor," says Fazila. "But when I'm at Skateistan, I'm in a nice place."

Reading

1 Read Fazila's profile. Answer the questions.

1 How old is Fazila?
2 Where does she come from?

2 Read about Fazila. Are the statements
1.32 true (T) or false (F)?

1 Fazila lives in Afghanistan. *T*
2 There aren't any classrooms in Skateistan.
3 Children can study English at Skateistan.
4 Boys and girls work together in schools in Afghanistan.
5 Fazila has a skateboard.
6 Fazila is happy at school.

Class discussion

- Can you skateboard?
- Do you think Skateistan is a good idea? Why?/Why not?
- Would you like a skateboarding school in your town?
- What special schools are there in your country?

3 School Days

Vocabulary • Daily routines

Grammar
Present simple:
affirmative and negative;
Present simple: questions

Vocabulary
Daily routines;
School subjects

Speaking
Time

Writing
An email

Word list page 43
Workbook page 106

1 Match the pictures to these phrases. Then listen, check and repeat.
1.33

brush my teeth
clean up my room
do homework
get dressed
get up _1_
go home
go to bed
have breakfast
have dinner
have lunch
meet friends
start school
take a shower
watch TV

2 Complete the sentences with phrases from Exercise 1.

1 I *get up* in the morning, and I *take* a shower.
2 I .... breakfast, then I .... my teeth.
3 I .... my friends on the bus.
4 I start .... at 9:00 a.m. My favorite class is math.
5 We .... lunch at 1:00 p.m.
6 I .... my homework after school. I study in my room.
7 In the evening, I .... TV with my family.
8 We .... to bed at 10:30 p.m. on school days.
9 I .... my room on Saturdays.

3 What words can follow these verbs?

1 brush *my teeth*   2 have   3 get   4 go

4 In pairs, make a statement about your day. Your partner guesses *true* or *false*.

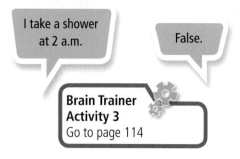

I take a shower at 2 a.m.

False.

Brain Trainer
Activity 3
Go to page 114

Reading

1 Look at Maisie's family photo. Answer the questions.

1 How many brothers does she have?
2 How many sisters does she have?
3 How many people are in her family?

2 Read and check your answers to Exercise 1.

3 Read Maisie's blog again. Put these things
1.34 in the order Maisie does them.

a play with brothers and sisters
b take a shower
c have breakfast *1*
d do homework
e go to school
f clean up the living room

4 Read Maisie's blog again. Complete the sentences.

1.34 1 Life in Maisie's house *is fun, but it's difficult, too.*
2 Maisie's family is .... .
3 Every morning, Maisie is in the bathroom for .... .
4 Maisie's parents don't have a car; they have .... .
5 Maisie has dinner at .... .
6 After 8 p.m., Maisie .... .

5 What about you? In pairs, ask and answer.

1 Do you have a big family?
2 How many brothers and sisters do you have?
3 Can you watch TV on school days?
4 Can you meet your friends after school?

> How many brothers and sisters do you have?

> I have two sisters.

A Day With ... My Big Family

My name is Maisie Hall, and I have five brothers and sisters! Life in our house is fun, but it's difficult, too.

On school days, I get up very early, at 6 a.m., but I don't take a shower right away. I have my breakfast first. Our family is big, so we don't have breakfast together. After breakfast I take a shower and get dressed. I only have five minutes in the bathroom before my sister knocks on the door!

At 8 a.m. we go to school in our minivan. It has ten seats, it's big, and it's fun!

School starts at 8:30 a.m., and we go home at 3 p.m. After school I don't watch TV. I clean up the living room for my mom, and I play with my brothers and sisters.

We have dinner all together at 6 p.m. My baby brother goes to bed at 7 p.m., and my other brothers and sisters go to bed at 8 p.m. Then I can work!

From 8 p.m. to 9 p.m. I do my homework, read a book or watch TV with my parents. After that I brush my teeth and go to bed.

Me and my family

Me

Grammar • Present simple: affirmative and negative

Affirmative		
I/You/We/They	get up	at 7 a.m.
He/She/It	gets up	

Negative		
I/You/We/They	don't (do not) get up	at 7 a.m.
He/She/It	doesn't (does not) get up	

Grammar reference Workbook page 90

Watch Out!
he / she / it → looks, watches, studies

1 Study the grammar table. Choose the correct options to complete the rules.

1 We add -s to the verb after *I, you, we, they* / *he, she, it*.
2 We use the words *don't* and *doesn't* to make the *affirmative* / *negative* of the Present simple.

Pronunciation -s endings

2a Listen to the -s endings.
1.35   likes → /s/   plays → /z/   watches → /ɪz/

b Listen and say /s/, /z/ or /ɪz/.
1.36
1 gets up   5 eats
2 has   6 dances
3 cleans   7 does
4 watches   8 goes

c Listen again and repeat.
1.36

3 Choose the correct options.

1 I *get* / *gets* up early and have breakfast.
2 My teachers *has* / *have* lunch at school.
3 They *has* / *have* dinner at 6 p.m.
4 We *goes* / *go* to the movies on Wednesdays.
5 Tom *meet* / *meets* his friends after school.
6 You *does* / *do* your homework before dinner.

4 Make negative sentences.

1 Josh has breakfast at 9 a.m.
   Josh doesn't have breakfast at 9 a.m.
2 Adam goes to school by train.
3 I do Sudokus.
4 Lorenzo and Tina have lunch at one o'clock.
5 Anita plays tennis on Saturdays.
6 Ella goes to bed at 9:30 p.m.
7 We have dinner together.
8 You speak Chinese.

5 Complete the descriptions. Then guess the person.

get dressed	~~get up~~	get up	go
have	not have	not get up	

1 Every Saturday I ¹ *get up* at 7 a.m., and I ² ....
in my old clothes. First, I clean out the barn
on our farm, and then the animals ³ ....
breakfast. My parents and I ⁴ .... breakfast
early. We eat eggs and toast at about 10 a.m.
2 I ⁵ .... early on Saturday. I watch TV in bed, and
I ⁶ .... at 11 a.m. In the afternoon, my friends
and I ⁷ .... to the park and play soccer. My dog,
Sunny, likes soccer, too!

6 What about you? Write affirmative and negative sentences about your weekend.

I watch TV on Saturday.

Vocabulary • School subjects

1 Match the pictures to these words. Then listen, check and repeat.

1.37

art	computer science	English	French
geography	history	literature	math *1*
music	PE	science	social studies

Word list page 43
Workbook page 106

2 Jimmy can't find the right classroom. Listen and say the class.

1.38

1 Classroom 1 *math*
2 Classroom 2
3 Classroom 3
4 Classroom 4
5 Classroom 5
6 Classroom 6

3 Match these activities to subjects from Exercise 1.

1 write essays
   literature, history …
2 speak in pairs
3 use a computer
4 move your body
5 work with numbers
6 sing
7 read books
8 draw or paint
9 work with maps
10 do experiments
11 talk about society
12 write stories

4 What about you? In pairs, ask and answer.

1 What classes do you have on Monday?
2 Who is your art teacher?
3 What days are your English classes?
4 Are you good at math?
5 Do you have PE today?
6 What is your favorite class?

What classes do you have on Monday?

I have history, math, English and PE.

Brain Trainer Activity 4
Go to page 114

Chatroom Time

Speaking and Listening

1 **Look at the photo.**

1 Where are Monica and Nick?

2 What objects can you see in the photo?

2 **Listen and read the conversation. Match**
1.39 **the phrases to make sentences.**

1 Monica meets Nick *b*

2 Monica gets up early

3 Monica lives

4 Nick has a

5 Nick's class starts

a on a farm.

b at a quarter past eight.

c at nine o'clock.

d because the bus leaves at seven fifteen.

e history class first.

3 **Act out the conversation in pairs.**

Monica	Hi, Nick! You're early.
Nick	Really? What time is it?
Monica	It's a quarter past eight.
Nick	Why are you early?
Monica	Because the bus from our town leaves at seven fifteen.
Nick	You're lucky to live on a farm. I love farms.
Monica	Yes, I know. Do you want to come over on Saturday?
Nick	Sure! Great idea! Thanks.
Monica	Great! What class do you have now?
Nick	I have history first.
Monica	What time does it start?
Nick	It starts at nine o'clock. What time is it?
Monica	It's eight twenty. See you later!

Say it in your language …

I know.

See you later!

4 Look back at the conversation. Find the times Nick and Monica talk about.

1 a quarter past eight …

5 Read the phrases for asking and answering about time.

Asking about time	Answering about time
What time is it?	It's a quarter past eight.
What time does it start?	It's eight twenty.
What time does it finish?	At seven fifteen.
	It starts at nine o'clock.
	It ends at half past one.

6 What time is it?

1 7:15 *It's a quarter past seven. / It's seven fifteen.*
2 11:25
3 8:05
4 2:50
5 3:30

7 Listen to the conversation. Act out
1.40 the conversation in pairs.

Girl What time is it?
Boy It's [1] a quarter past eleven.
Girl What time is our [2] French class?
Boy It starts at [3] eleven twenty. We're early.
Girl What time does it end?
Boy It ends at [4] twelve ten.

8 Work in pairs. Replace the words in purple in Exercise 7 with these words. Act out the conversation.

> What time is it?   It's a quarter past eight.

1 eleven o'clock / five past eleven / half past eleven

2 English / geography / science / math

3 twelve o'clock / twenty-five past twelve / twelve forty-five

4 twelve forty-five / one o'clock / one thirty

9 Act out the conversation again with your own words and ideas.

Grammar • Present simple: questions and short answers

Questions		
Do I/you/we/they	get up	at seven o'clock?
Does he/she/it	get up	
Short answers		

Yes, I/you/we/they do.
No, I/you/we/they don't.

Yes, he/she/it does.
No, he/she/it doesn't.

Grammar reference Workbook page 90

1 Study the grammar table. Complete the rules.

1 Present simple questions start with *Do* or ….. .
2 Short answers with *Yes* end with *do* or ….. .
3 Short answers with *No* end with *don't* or ….. .

2 Choose the correct options to make questions. Then write answers.

1 *Do / Does* Nick and Monica get up early?
Do Nick and Monica get up early? Yes, they do.
2 *Do / Does* they go to the same school?
3 *Do / Does* Monica walk to school?
4 *Do / Does* Monica live on a farm?
5 *Do / Does* Nick have history first?

3 Make questions for these answers.

1 No, I don't speak German.
Do you speak German?
2 No, we don't live in Houston.
3 Yes, she goes to school by bus.
4 Yes, we write essays in English.
5 No, I don't. I have lunch at 2 p.m.
6 Yes, he studies French.

4 Make questions. In pairs, ask and answer.

1 you / get up / at half past six?
Do you get up at half past six? No, I don't.
2 you / go to school / at 7:15?
3 your friend / like / math?
4 your teacher / watch TV / after school?
5 you and your family / have dinner together?
6 you / go to bed / at ten thirty?
7 your friends / bike to school?

Reading

1 **Look quickly at the quiz. Can you find this information?**

1 Eight countries.
2 The names of two schools.

The Big School Quiz

Do you know about schools in other countries?
Take this quiz and find out!

1 The City Montessori School in Lucknow, India, is very big. How many students study there?
a 12,000
b 22,000
c More than 39,000

2 In France, some students never go to school on …
a Saturdays and Sundays.
b Wednesdays and Sundays.
c Sundays and Mondays.

3 In Sweden, Switzerland and Denmark, some children start school at …
a 7 years old.
b 8 years old.
c 9 years old.

4 In South Korea, some students stay at school after classes end at 4 p.m. Do they …
a do their homework?
b clean up their classrooms?
c watch TV?

5 Australian children go to school 200 days a year. How many days a year do Chinese children go to school?
a 211 days a year
b 231 days a year
c 251 days a year

6 Shishi Middle School in China is about …
a one thousand years old.
b three thousand years old.
c two thousand years old.

7 In China, some children finish school at …
a 12 years old.
b 15 years old.
c 16 years old.

Answer key

1c 2b 3a 4a 5c 6c 7b

Key Words

find out   to stay   thousand

2 **Take the quiz. Then listen and check your answers.**
1.41

3 **Now read about your score.**

0 – 2 Uh oh! Find out about other countries.
3 – 5 Well done. You know some interesting facts.
6 – 7 Excellent!

4 **Read the quiz again. Name the countries.**
1.41
1 There is a 2,000-year-old school in this country. *China*
2 The school day ends at 4 p.m. in this country.
3 The City Montessori School is in this country.
4 Children go to school for 200 days a year in this country.
5 Students can finish school when they are 15 in this country.
6 Some children start school at 7 years old in these three countries.

Listening

1 **Listen to an interview. Put the topics in order 1–3.**
1.42
a summer
b clothes
c break

2 **Listen again. Correct the sentences.**
1.42
1 Jin goes to school in Japan.
2 His school day ends at 4 p.m.
3 He has one hour for his lunch break.
4 He wears a blue shirt and blue pants.
5 He exercises on Monday and Thursday.
6 He doesn't study in summer.

3 **Listen again. Swap books and check**
1.42 **your partner's answers.**

Writing • An email

1 **Read the Writing File.**

2 **Read the email. Find time phrases with *on*, *in* and *at*.**

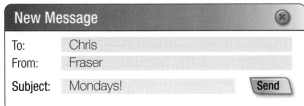

New Message   ⊗

To: Chris
From: Fraser

Subject: Mondays!   Send

Hi Chris,

Hurray! It's Monday again. It's my favorite school day! Do you know why? Because we have a French class (at) five past nine on Monday, and we have "petit déjeuner" (breakfast) in the class. I love croissants!

Then we have a double math class in the morning, but that's OK because our math teacher is very funny, and I'm good at math!

Our music classes are at a quarter past two, and they're fun. Music is my favorite class because the teacher, Mr. Singer, is crazy! He doesn't talk in his classes—he sings all the time!

What about you? Do you like Mondays?

Bye for now,

Fraser

3 **Read the email again. Answer the questions.**
1 Does Fraser like Mondays? *Yes, he does.*
2 What time is Fraser's French class?
3 Does Fraser have math on Mondays?
4 Is Fraser good at math?
5 Who is Fraser's music teacher?
6 What does the music teacher do?

4 **Choose the correct options.**
1 I have English *in / at* the morning.
2 Our art class is *at / on* Friday.
3 My school day starts *in / at* eight o'clock.
4 We have PE *in / on* the afternoon.

5 **Think about your favorite school day. Answer the questions.**
1 What is your favorite day?
2 What classes do you have on your favorite day?
3 Who are your teachers? What subjects do they teach?
4 What time are your classes?
5 What is your favorite class?

6 **Write a short email about your favorite school day. Use "My email" and your answers from Exercise 5.**

My email
1 Start your email.
   Dear/Hi … ,
2 Say what your favorite day is.
   My favorite day is … .
3 Say what classes you have.
   We have … on … .
4 Say who your teachers are and what subjects they teach.
5 Say what time your classes are.
6 Say what your favorite class is and why.
   … is my favorite class because … .
7 Finish your email.
   See you soon! / Bye for now!

Remember!
- Use time phrases to describe when things happen.
- Use the Present simple.
- Use the vocabulary in this unit.
- Check your grammar, spelling and punctuation.

Refresh Your Memory!

Grammar • Review

1 **Make sentences. Use the Present simple affirmative.**

1 Linda / watch / TV before school.
   Linda watches TV before school.
2 Max / study / French / in college.
3 Eva and Sara / study / math.
4 My dad / clean up / the house every evening.
5 My brother / play / soccer in the backyard.
6 You / get up / before me.

2 **Complete the sentences with the Present simple negative.**

1 I get up early, but Adam .... .
   I get up early, but Adam *doesn't get up early.*
2 You like history, but Nadia .... .
3 I have lunch at school, but Mom and Dad .... .
4 We walk to school, but Maria and Anna .... .
5 I go to bed at 10 p.m., but my sister .... .
6 I do my homework in front of the TV, but you .... .

3 **Complete the email with *do*, *don't*, *does* or *doesn't*.**

Hi Marta,

What subjects [1] *do* you study at school? We can choose subjects now because we are fourteen. I [2] .... have history classes now, but I study geography. I [3] .... study art because I can't paint. My friend Matt [4] .... like French, so his language class is German. [5] .... your school give you a choice? At what age [6] .... you choose? Write and tell me!

Veronica

4 **Match the questions to the correct answers.**

1 Does Alan like dogs? *b*
2 Do you walk to school?
3 Do I start school before you?
4 Do Pepe and Nina read books in English?
5 Does Angela meet her friends before school?

a Yes, they do.
b No, he doesn't.
c Yes, she does.
d Yes, I do.
e No, you don't.

Vocabulary • Review

5 **Complete the routine verbs.**

Dan gets [1] *up* at 6 every morning. He doesn't [2] .... dressed or [3] .... his teeth, and he doesn't [4] .... a shower. He [5] .... breakfast, but he doesn't [6] .... TV, and he doesn't [7] .... homework. He [8] .... to bed when he wants to. Why? Because Dan is my dog!

6 **Match the definitions to these words.**

art	computer science	English	~~French~~
geography	literature	music	PE

1 They speak this language in France. *French*
2 We learn about the world and other countries in this class.
3 We play soccer and basketball in this class.
4 This class teaches us about books, stories and poems.
5 We paint pictures in this class.
6 We learn about computers in this class.
7 They speak this language in the US.
8 We play instruments in this class.

Speaking • Review

7 **Put the sentences in the correct order. Then listen and check.**
1.43

a It starts at eleven fifteen. We're early.
b What time is it? *1*
c What time does it end?
d Oh. What time is our French class?
e It ends at twelve twenty.
f It's ten ten.

Dictation

8 **Listen and write in your notebook.**
1.44

9 **Swap books and check your partner's work.**

✓ **My assessment profile:** Workbook page 129

Technology File

How to Make a Camera Obscura

What you need ...

- a tube – for example, an old chips tube
- a ruler
- scissors
- some aluminum foil
- a needle
- some adhesive tape
- some black paint and a paintbrush
- tracing paper
- two big rubber bands

1 Eat the chips! Then clean the inside of the tube and paint it black inside and outside.

2 Draw a line around the tube 5 cm from the bottom. Then cut along the line. You now have two tubes—one short tube and one long tube.

3 With the needle, make a hole at the bottom of the short tube.

4 Tape some tracing paper on the top of the short tube. Then tape the short tube and the long tube together again. The tracing paper is now in the middle of the tube.

5 Put the aluminum foil all around the tube and attach with rubber bands.

6 Go outside. Close one eye. Put the tube over the other eye. Hold your hand up to the sky and point the tube at it.

7 The light comes through the pinhole and makes a color image on the tracing paper. What is strange about the image?

Reading

1 Read the text quickly. Put the pictures in the correct order.

1 b

2 Read the text again. Answer the questions.

1.45
1 What color do you paint the tube? *black*
2 Do you cut around the top or the bottom of the tube?
3 How do you make the hole in the tube?
4 What do you put around the tube?
5 How do you look through the camera?
6 Where do you see the image when you use a Camera Obscura?

My Technology File

3 In pairs, make a Camera Obscura.

4 Write two sentences about the image on the tracing paper.

Review 1

Grammar • Have

1 **Complete the sentences with *has* or *have*.**

1 He *has* seven brothers.
2 They .... a black-and-white dog.
3 It .... big teeth.
4 I .... my cell phone.
5 She .... a big house.
6 We .... a good French teacher.

2 **Put the sentences in Exercise 1 in the negative.**

1 *He doesn't have seven brothers.*

3 **Complete the conversation.**

A ¹ *Do* you ² .... a TV in your bedroom?
B No, I ³ ...., but I ⁴ .... a laptop. I watch my sister's DVDs on it.
A ⁵ .... your sister have a lot of DVDs?
B Yes, she ⁶ ...., but she doesn't ⁷ .... the new Robert Pattinson movie.
A ⁸ .... they have it in stores now?
B Yes, they ⁹ .... . I love Robert Pattinson!

• Possessive 's

4 **Copy the sentences. Add an apostrophe in the correct place.**

1 My dad's shoes are horrible.
2 Her sisters names are Kate and Lianne.
3 This towns shopping mall is boring.
4 I like Sams parents.
5 They're Stan and Sophies friends.
6 All the teachers cars are in front of the school.

• Possessive adjectives

5 **Complete the second sentence so it has a similar meaning to the first sentence.**

1 I have a green bag.
  My bag is green.
2 She has an interesting book.
  .... book is interesting.
3 It has awesome pictures.
  .... pictures are awesome.
4 They have a good camera.
  .... camera is good.

• There is/There are; Some/Any

6 **Complete the questions about Allendale. Then answer them using the information from the table.**

1 Are there any houses? *Yes, there are.*
2 .... a post office? .... .
3 .... any banks? .... .
4 .... a movie theater? .... .
5 .... a park? .... .
6 .... any schools? .... .

WHAT'S IN ALLENDALE?			
houses	800	stores	4
schools	2	lakes	✗
banks	✗	a museum	✓
a park	✓	cafés	6
a post office	✓	a sports complex	✗
a movie theater	✗	a library	✗

7 **The information in this paragraph is not correct. Rewrite the paragraph correctly.**

There aren't any stores in Allendale, but there are some lakes. There are some museums, and there's a café. There's a sports complex, and there's a library.

There are some stores in Allendale, but … .

• *Can/Can't* for ability

8 **Make sentences with *can/can't*.**

1 I / climb / trees / ✓
  I can climb trees.
2 My dad / dance / ✗
3 My friends / juggle / ✓
4 You / skate / ✗
5 We / bike / to school / ✓
6 The baby / walk / ✗

9 **Make questions. Then answer.**

1 Lady Gaga / sing / Can / ?
  Can Lady Gaga sing? Yes, she can.
2 dogs / fly / Can / ?
3 you / Can / in English / write / ?
4 Can / run / fast / good soccer players / ?

• Present simple

10 **Complete the text with the Present simple form of the verbs.**

I ¹ *live* (live) in Australia. My home is 200 km from a town, so I ² .... (not go) to school every day. I ³ .... (have) classes on the Internet. My brother ⁴ .... (not live) at home from Monday to Friday. He ⁵ .... (stay) at his school, and we only ⁶ .... (see) him on the weekend. After his classes, he ⁷ .... (study) with his friends.

11 **Look at the information. Then complete the sentences.**

On Fridays at ...	4 o'clock	5 o'clock	6 o'clock
Maria and Dan	play soccer	do homework	meet friends
Jacob	clean up the classroom	go to the park	have dinner

1 Maria and Dan *don't meet* friends at 4 o'clock.
2 Jacob .... the classroom at 4 o'clock.
3 Maria and Dan .... homework at 5 o'clock.
4 Jacob .... to the park at 6 o'clock.
5 Maria and Dan .... soccer at 6 o'clock.

12 **Make questions. Then answer using the information from Exercise 11.**

1 Jacob / have dinner / at 5 o'clock / ?
  Does Jacob have dinner at 5 o'clock?
  No, he doesn't.
2 he / clean up the classroom / at 4 o'clock / ?
3 Maria and Dan / play soccer / at 6 o'clock / ?
4 they / go to the park / at 5 o'clock / ?
5 Jacob / do homework / at 6 o'clock / ?

13 **Make questions.**

1 No, I don't. (have breakfast at school)
  Do you have breakfast at school?
2 Yes, we do. (walk to school)
3 No, she doesn't. (read a lot of books)
4 Yes, it does. (start at half past nine)
5 No, I don't. (get up at six o'clock)

Speaking • Talking about position

1 **Look at the picture and complete the sentences with these words.**

behind	in	in front of	next to	~~on~~	under

1 The laptop is *on* the desk.
2 The cell phone is .... the laptop.
3 The backpack is .... the laptop.
4 The guitar is .... the backpack.
5 The ball is .... the desk.
6 The skateboard is .... the ball.

• Orders and warnings

2 **Match the beginnings (1–5) to the endings (a–e) of the teacher's instructions.**

1 Open ——— a down!
2 Stand ——— b your books.
3 Be   c quiet!
4 Sit   d up!
5 Don't   e shout in class.

• Time

3 **Make questions. Then look at the clocks and write the answers.**

1 does / What time / start / it / ?
  What time does it start?
  It starts at a quarter to four/three forty-five.
2 is / time / What / it / ?
3 end / time / What / it / does / ?

Vocabulary • Objects

1 **Complete the sentences with these words.**

DVD	game console	~~guitar~~
laptop	magazines	MP3 player
posters	wallet	watch

1 My brother can play the *guitar*. He's very good!
2 I read a lot of ..... .
3 I don't have a ..... . What time is it?
4 Do you do your homework on a .... ?
5 Do you have any good music on your .... ?
6 I only have one dollar in my ..... .
7 Can you play *MotorMania* on that .... ?
8 I have ten .... on my bedroom walls.
9 Can we watch a .... ?

• Adjectives

2 **Complete the words.**

1 He's a g <u>o o d</u> actor, but I don't like his movies.
2 A lot of people play soccer. It's very p_ _ _ _ar.
3 You can do today's homework in 15 minutes. It's e_ _ _ .
4 What?! $35 for a pen?! That's very e_ _ _ns_ _ _.
5 Our car's very o_ _, but we like it.
6 She has a sm_ _ _ dog in her bag. Look!
7 I play tennis, but I'm a very b_ _ player.
8 That watch is very ch _ _ _, only $5.
9 Don't watch that DVD. It's b_ _ i _ _.
10 Her classes are very in_ _ _ _ _ _ng.

• Places in a town

3 **Match the beginnings (1–8) to the endings (a–h) of the sentences.**

1 Send a letter at
2 You can see old things at
3 You can find new clothes at
4 There are a lot of dollars at
5 You can eat at
6 Dogs and people walk in
7 There are a lot of books at
8 You can watch movies at

a the bank.
b the movie theater.
c the shopping mall.
d the post office.
e the museum.
f the café.
g the park.
h the library.

• Action verbs

4 **Complete the sentences with these words.**

bike	climb	fly	juggle
jump	play	run	~~walk~~

1 My friends *walk* to school.
2 I.... to school on my mountain bike.
3 My grandma can .... ten kilometers.
4 My grandpa can .... six balls.
5 People often .... to Greece on vacation.
6 I can't .... soccer.
7 She can .... very high.
8 Can you .... this tree?

• Daily routines

5 **Complete the sentences with these words.**

bed	breakfast	brush	clean up
dinner	dressed	~~get~~	go
homework	lunch	meet	shower
start	watch		

I [1] *get* up at seven o'clock. Then I get [2] .... in my school uniform, have [3] .... (eggs and toast!) and [4] .... my teeth. I [5] .... school at nine o'clock. I have [6] .... at school. After school, I [7] .... my friends in the park. Next, I [8] .... home, do all my [9] .... and [10] .... TV. Then I have [11] .... . My favorite is pizza! I take a [12] .... after that. Then I [13] .... my room and go to [14] ..... .

• School subjects

6 **Complete the school subjects.**

1 m a t <u>h</u>
2 m u _ _ _
3 F _ _ _ c h
4 E _ _ _ _ s h
5 h _ s t _ _ _
6 s c _ _ n _ _
7 l i t _ _ _ t u r e
8 g _ _ g r _ _ _ y
9 c _ _ _ _ _ er sc _ _ _ c _

Word list

Unit 1 • My World

Objects

camera	/ˈkæmərə/
cell phone	/ˈsɛl foʊn/
comics	/ˈkamɪks/
DVD	/diːviːˈdiː/
game console	/ˈgeɪm ˈkɑnsoʊl/
guitar	/gɪˈtɑr/
ice skates	/ˈaɪs skeɪts/
laptop	/ˈlæptɑp/
magazine	/ˌmægəˈzin/
MP3 player	/ɛmpi θri ˈpleɪɚ/
poster	/ˈpoʊstɚ/
skateboard	/ˈskeɪtbɔrd/
wallet	/ˈwɑlɪt/
watch	/wɑtʃ/

Adjectives

bad	/bæd/
big	/bɪg/
boring	/ˈbɔrɪŋ/
cheap	/tʃip/
difficult	/ˈdɪfɪkəlt/
easy	/ˈizi/
expensive	/ɪkˈspɛnsɪv/
good	/gʊd/
interesting	/ˈɪntrɪstɪŋ, ˈɪntəˌrɛstɪŋ/
new	/nu/
old	/oʊld/
popular	/ˈpɑpyələ/
small	/smɔl/
unpopular	/ʌnˈpɑpyələ/

Unit 2 • Around Town

Places in a town

bank	/bæŋk/
bus station	/ˈbʌs ˈsteɪʃən/
café	/kæˈfeɪ/
hospital	/ˈhɑspɪtl/
library	/ˈlaɪbrɛri/
movie theater	/ˈmuvi ˈθiətɚ/
museum	/mjuːˈziːəm/
park	/pɑrk/
police station	/pəˈlis ˈsteɪʃən/
post office	/ˈpoʊst ˈɔfɪs/
shopping mall	/ˈʃɑpɪŋ mɔl/
sports complex	/ˈspɔrts ˌkɑmplɛks/
town square	/ˈtaʊn ˈskwɛr/
train station	/ˈtreɪn ˈsteɪʃən/

Action verbs

bike	/baɪk/
climb	/klaɪm/
dance	/dæns/
fly	/flaɪ/
juggle	/ˈdʒʌgəl/
jump	/dʒʌmp/
play	/pleɪ/
run	/rʌn/
sing	/sɪŋ/
skate	/skeɪt/
swim	/swɪm/
walk	/wɔk/

Unit 3 • School Days

Daily routines

brush my teeth	/ˈbrʌʃ maɪ ˈtiθ/
clean up my room	/ˈklin ʌp maɪ ˈrum/
do homework	/ˈdu ˈhoʊmwɚk/
get dressed	/ˈget ˈdrɛst/
get up	/ˈget ʌp/
go home	/ˈgoʊ ˈhoʊm/
go to bed	/ˈgoʊ tə ˈbɛd/
have breakfast	/ˈhæv ˈbrɛkfəst/
have dinner	/ˈhæv ˈdɪnɚ/
have lunch	/ˈhæv ˈlʌntʃ/
meet friends	/ˈmit ˈfrɛndz/
start school	/ˈstɑrt ˈskul/
take a shower	/ˈteɪk ə ˈʃaʊɚ/
watch TV	/ˈwɑtʃ ˌtiˈvi/

School subjects

art	/ɑrt/
computer science	/kəmˈpyutɚ ˈsaɪəns/
English	/ˈɪŋglɪʃ/
French	/frɛntʃ/
geography	/dʒiˈɑgrəfi/
history	/ˈhɪstəri/
literature	/ˈlɪtərətʃə/
math	/ˈmæθ/
music	/ˈmyuzɪk/
PE	/piˈi/
science	/ˈsaɪəns/
social studies	/ˈsoʊʃəl ˈsaɪəns/

Grammar
Adverbs of frequency;
Present simple with *Wh*
questions; *Must/Mustn't*

Vocabulary
Unusual animals;
Parts of the body

Speaking
Likes and dislikes

Writing
An animal fact sheet

Word list page 77
Workbook page 107

Vocabulary • Unusual animals

1 **Match the pictures to these words. Then listen, check and repeat.**

2.1

frog
giant rabbit
hissing cockroach
lizard
parrot *1*
piranha
pygmy goat
python
stick insect
tarantula

2 **Find one animal in Exercise 1 for each of these categories. Then think of two more.**

1 fish *piranha, ..., ,*
2 spider
3 bird
4 amphibian
5 reptile
6 mammal
7 insect

3 **In pairs, read the clues and guess the animal.**

1 It can fly. *a bird*
2 It's green. It lives in water. It eats insects.
3 It can swim, but it can't walk.
4 It lives under the ground. It eats vegetables.
   It's a popular pet.
5 It makes a loud noise. It's an insect.
6 It can't walk, and it can't fly, but it can
   climb trees.
7 People drink its milk.
8 It can say words.

4 **Think of an animal. In pairs, ask and answer.**

Can it fly?

Yes, it can.

Is it a parrot?

Yes, it is.

Brain Trainer
Activity 4
Go to page 115

Reading

1 Look at the photos. What do you think the text is about?

   a An article about tarantulas.
   b A text about life in a zoo.
   c A blog about animals.

2 Read the text and check your answers to Exercise 1.

3 Read the text again. Answer the questions.

2.2
   1 What's Tom's job? *He's a zookeeper.*
   2 When does Tom get up?
   3 When does he start work?
   4 Where do the hissing cockroaches come from?
   5 Where does the tarantula come from?
   6 What animals is Tom scared of?
   7 What does Tom think about his job?

4 Read the text again. Are the statements true (T) or false (F)?

2.2
   1 Tom feeds the animals in the morning. *F*
   2 Tom sometimes hides the hissing cockroaches' food in different places.
   3 Tiny is only ten years old.
   4 Visitors to the zoo are scared of the red-knee tarantula.
   5 Tom enjoys his job because he can learn more about animals.
   6 Tom isn't tired at the end of the day.

5 What about you? **In pairs, ask and answer.**

   1 Which animals do you like/dislike?
   2 What unusual animals do you know of?
   3 Are you scared of spiders or insects?

> Do you like animals?

> I love animals, but I'm scared of reptiles.

A Day in the Life ...

Tom works in the Unusual Pets section of Bemidji Animal Park in Minnesota. He is a zookeeper. We talk to him about a typical day.

Describe a typical day at the zoo.

I get up at 6:30, and I start work at 8 o'clock. I usually put on my boots because it's often very dirty in the animal enclosures. I clean the animal enclosures every day, and in the afternoon I feed the animals. I'm always busy! I never finish work before 5:30.

What animals do you like, and what animals do you dislike?

I love the hissing cockroaches! They come from Madagascar, and they're very noisy. I sometimes hide their food in different places. It's a game for them! But I don't like the tarantulas. We have a red-knee tarantula from Mexico. Her name's Tiny, and she's twenty-five years old. Visitors to the zoo love her, but I'm scared of spiders. I hardly ever work with them.

Why do you like your job?

I work with great people, and I learn new things about animals every day. At the end of the day, I'm often tired, but my job is always interesting.

Grammar • Adverbs of frequency

0% 10%	25% 50%	80% 100%
never / hardly ever	sometimes / often	usually / always
I hardly ever work with them.	I'm often very tired.	My job is always interesting.

1 Study the grammar table. Choose the correct options to complete the rule.

> Adverbs come *before* / *after* the verb *to be* and *before* / *after* most other verbs.

2 Put the adverbs in the correct place.

1 We go to the zoo on the weekend. (sometimes)
We sometimes go to the zoo on the weekend.
2 My English class is interesting. (usually)
3 My parrot watches TV in the morning. (often)
4 My dad is happy on Friday evening. (always)
5 I bike to school. (never)
6 You take our dog for a walk. (hardly ever)

3 Put the words in the correct order to make sentences.

1 often / Tom / very / is / tired / work / After
After work Tom is often very tired.
2 trees / sometimes / Goats / climb
3 eighteen / Cats / sleep / often / hours / for
4 after / feed / rabbit / my / usually / I / school
5 ever / Sarah / her / hardly / parrot / talks / to

4 Look at the chart and complete the sentences.

On the weekend	Peter	Abby
1 play soccer	100%	50%
2 play computer games	80%	10%
3 do homework	80%	100%
4 listen to music	0%	80%

1 Peter *always* plays soccer on the weekend.
Abby *often plays soccer on the weekend.*
2 Peter .... plays computer games on the weekend.
Abby .... .
3 Peter .... does his homework on the weekend.
Abby .... .
4 Peter .... listens to music on the weekend.
Abby .... .

• Present simple with *Wh* questions

Wh questions	
Where do you live?	In Manchester.
When do you finish school?	At four o'clock.
What does she eat for breakfast?	Cereal.
Who does Mrs. West teach?	8th grade students.
Why do you walk to school?	Because we don't have a car.
How often do you play football?	Every day!

Grammar reference Workbook page 92

5 Study the grammar table. Choose the correct options to complete the rules.

1 We use *who* to ask about *people* / *things*.
2 We use *what* to ask about *people* / *things*.
3 We use *when* to ask about *place* / *time*.
4 We use *where* to ask about *place* / *time*.

6 Match the questions to the answers.

1 How often do elephants eat?
2 Who is your favorite singer?
3 When is your birthday?
4 What is in your schoolbag?
5 Why do you take the bus?
6 Where do piranhas live?

a Ariana Grande.
b It's on June 17.
c Because we don't have a car.
d They live in South American rivers.
e They eat every three hours.
f Two pens, a ruler and a book about spiders.

7 What about you? Make questions. In pairs, ask and answer.

Where do you live?   I live in San Jose.

1 Where / you / live?
2 Who / your / best friend?
3 How often / you / play sports?
4 What / your / favorite animal?
5 What / you / usually / do / on the weekend?
6 How often / you / go / to the zoo?

Vocabulary • Parts of the body

1 **Label the picture with these words. Then listen,**
2.3 **check and repeat.**

arm	beak *1*	fin	finger	foot	hand	head
leg	neck	paw	tail	toe	wing	

Word list page 77
Workbook page 107

2 **What parts of the body do we have? Complete**
the sentences with words from Exercise 1.

1 We have **zero** *tails.*
2 We have **one** .... .
3 We have **two** .... .
4 We have **ten** .... .

3 **What animal is it? Read the clues and guess.**

bird	~~fish~~	pygmy goat	hissing cockroach	spider

1 It doesn't have legs. It has a head. It doesn't
have arms. It has fins. *It's a fish.*
2 It has six legs. It has a head. It doesn't have
a neck.
3 It has eight legs. It doesn't have a tail.
4 It has two legs. It has a tail. It doesn't have
arms. It has wings and a beak.
5 It has four legs and a tail. It doesn't have fins.

4 **Complete the descriptions with these words.**
2.4 **Then listen and check.**

beak	bird	eyes	head
insects	~~legs~~	tail	wings

The wolf spider is an unusual pet. It has eight
¹ *legs*, and it can run and jump. It also has
eight ² .... , and it can see in the dark. The wolf
spider's ³ .... is small, but its body is large. It eats
⁴ .... .

A cockatiel is a ⁵ .... .
It has a yellow, gray
or white head, with a
small ⁶ .... . Its ⁷ .... are
usually gray and white,
and it has a long black
or gray ⁸ .... .
Cockatiels are from
Australia, but they are
popular pets around
the world.

Brain Trainer
Activity 5
Go to page 115

Chatroom Likes and dislikes

Speaking and Listening

1 **Look at the photos. Answer the questions.**

1 Where are the children?
2 What animals can you see?
3 Do you think Nick is angry or happy?

2 **Listen and read the conversation. Are the statements true (T) or false (F)?**

2.5

1 Sunny mustn't be on a leash on the farm. *F*
2 Sunny doesn't like running around the farm.
3 Monica likes living on a farm.
4 Monica likes getting up early.
5 Leo doesn't like getting up early.
6 Leo wants to feed the animals.
7 Monica's goats don't like eating Sunny's leash.

3 **Act out the conversation in groups of four.**

Monica	Hi, guys! Nick, you must put Sunny on a leash, please.
Nick	Sorry, Monica. Sunny loves running around the farm.
Julia	Do you like living on a farm, Monica?
Monica	Yes, I do, but I hate getting up early in the morning.
Leo	Me too! I don't like getting up early either.
Julia	That's true! On the weekend, you don't get up before 11!
Leo	I love feeding the animals. Look! I have some candy for them.
Monica	No, don't give them unhealthy food, Leo.
Leo	Sorry!
Nick	Sunny! Come here. You mustn't run away.
Monica	That's strange. Where's Sunny's leash?
Nick	I don't know.
Julia	Monica, what do your goats like eating?
Monica	They like eating everything!
Leo	Look! They love eating Sunny's leash!

Say it in your language …
Hi, guys!
Me too!

4 **Look back at the conversation. Find another way of saying …**

1 *like* doing something
2 *don't like* doing something

5 **Read the phrases for expressing likes and dislikes.**

Likes	Dislikes
Sunny loves running around the farm.	I hate getting up early.
They like eating everything.	I don't like getting up early.

Pronunciation Contrastive stress

6a **Listen. Which words are stressed?**

2.6

1 **A** I love playing basketball.
  B Do you? I don't. I love playing computer games.
2 **A** Joe hates getting up early.
  B No, Joe loves getting up early. Emma hates getting up early.

b **Listen again and repeat.**
2.6

---

7 **Listen to the conversations. Act out**
2.7 **the conversations in pairs.**

Nick	I love [1] watching animal shows on TV.
Julia	I don't.
Nick	I hate [2] getting up early!
Julia	Me too!
Julia	I like [3] cooking!
Leo	I don't.

8 **Work in pairs. Replace the words in purple in Exercise 7. Use these words and/or your own ideas. Act out the conversations.**

> I love watching TV. Me too!

1 go to the movies / go to the theater
2 go to bed early / stay up late
3 sing / juggle

Grammar • Must/Mustn't

Affirmative
I/You/He/She/It/We/They must get up early.

Negative
I/You/He/She/It/We/They mustn't get up late.

Grammar reference Workbook page 92

1 **Study the grammar table. Choose the correct option, 1 or 2, to complete the rule.**

> We use *must* and *mustn't* to talk about …
> 1 likes and dislikes.   2 important rules.

2 **Choose *must* or *mustn't* for these school rules.**

1 Students *must* / *mustn't* be late for school.
2 Students *must* / *mustn't* eat food in class.
3 Students *must* / *mustn't* listen to the teacher.
4 Students *must* / *mustn't* do their homework.
5 Students *must* / *mustn't* use cell phones in class.

3 **Look at the farm notice. Make sentences with *you must* and *you mustn't*.**

1 *You must be kind to the animals.*

Visitors to the Farm

✓	✗
1 Be kind to the animals	4 Hurt the animals
2 Close the gates	5 Give candy to the animals
3 Keep your dog on a leash	6 Climb the trees

Reading

1 Look at the text. Match the animals to their homes.

1 parrot   a tank
2 tarantula   b hutch
3 rabbit   c cage

Unusual Pets

This week three readers tell us about their unusual pets.

My pet is a red-and-blue parrot. She's 25, but she isn't old. Parrots often live for 70 years! She's from Africa, and her name is Miki. She lives in a cage in my bedroom. Miki likes talking and singing songs. Parrots are friendly birds, and Miki loves being with people. When she sees my friends, she always says, "Hi, guys!"
Rashid

Boris has eight legs. His body is black, and his legs are black and white. He's a Costa Rican zebra tarantula from Central America. Boris eats small insects, and he lives in a tank with some twigs and pieces of wood. There's also a small box in his tank because Boris loves hiding. Spiders like hot, humid places, so Boris's tank is 22–30ºC, and there's always a bowl of water there.
Lacey

Clarence is a British giant rabbit. He weighs 7.5 kilos, and he eats a lot! He sleeps in a hutch in my bedroom. He loves playing under my bed, but sometimes he eats my socks. When he's in the backyard, he likes digging. His favorite food is grass, but he also loves eating carrots!
Katie

Key Words

twig	to hide	humid
to weigh	to dig	grass

2 Read the text and check your answers to Exercise 1.

3 Read the text again. Write *Boris*, *Miki* or *Clarence*.
2.8
1 This pet likes hiding. *Boris*
2 This pet is red and blue.
3 This pet likes eating socks and carrots.
4 This pet eats insects.
5 This pet is sometimes outside.
6 This pet likes singing songs.

4 Read the text again. Answer the questions.
2.8
1 Where is Boris from?
Boris is from Central America.
2 Is Boris's tank hot or cold?
3 Is Miki old?
4 What does Miki say when she sees Rashid's friends?
5 How much does Clarence weigh?
6 Where does Clarence sleep?

Listening

1 Listen to the interview with Anna. Why is Dickens
2.9 a special dog?

2 Listen again. Answer the questions.
2.9
1 Name four things that Dickens does in the movie.
a He .... a tree.
b He .... out of a car.
c He .... in the ocean.
d He .... with a cat.
2 Who teaches Dickens?
3 What does he love doing?

3 Listen again. Swap books and check your
2.9 partner's answers.

Writing • An animal fact sheet

1 Read the Writing File.

2 Find the key information in this article. Is the same information in the fact sheet?

Komodo Dragons

Appearance

Komodo dragons are very big lizards. They grow to 3 meters and weigh 90 kilos. They are usually brown or gray in color, and they have a small head, a long tail and four short legs.

Habitat

Komodo dragons are from Indonesia. They live in deserts and in tropical regions.

Diet

Komodo dragons like eating birds, mammals—for example, goats and deer—or other reptiles.

Other Facts

Komodo dragons can run fast, and they can climb trees. They dig holes in the ground and sleep in them because they can stay cool there.

Komodo Dragon:
fact sheet

Color: brown or gray
Length: 3 meters
Weight: 90 kilos
Country: Indonesia
Habitat: deserts and tropical regions
Diet: birds, mammals, e.g., goats, deer, reptiles
Other facts: can run fast & climb trees; dig holes & sleep in them – stay cool

3 Copy the sentences. Rewrite them as notes.

1 Komodo dragons have very strong legs, and they can climb trees.
   Komodo dragons v strong legs; can climb trees
2 Spiders eat insects. They catch them in their webs.
3 Snakes can't run or walk, but they can swim.

4 Read the fact sheet again. Answer the questions.

1 How heavy are Komodo dragons?
   They weigh 90 kilos.
2 What color are they?
3 What country do they come from?
4 What do they eat?
5 Where do they sleep?

5 Think of an unusual animal and take notes to complete the fact sheet.

My Unusual Animal
fact sheet

Color: ....
Length: ....
Weight: ....
Country: ....
Habitat: ....
Diet: ....
Other facts: ....

6 Write a short article about your animal. Use the model from Exercise 2 and your notes from Exercise 5.

My unusual animal

1 **Appearance**
   They are … . (color / length / weight)
2 **Habitat**
   They live in … . (place / country)
3 **Diet**
   They eat … . (animals / plants)
4 **Other facts**
   They can … . (run / fly / swim / climb / jump)

Remember!
- Include the key information from your notes.
- Use the vocabulary in this unit.
- Check your grammar, spelling and punctuation.

Refresh Your Memory!

Grammar • Review

1 Copy and complete the frequency line with these adverbs.

always	hardly ever	~~never~~	often

0%	→	50%	→	100%
never	....	sometimes	....	usually	....

2 Put the words in the correct order to make sentences.

1 the / I / to / music / on / never / weekend / listen
I never listen to music on the weekend.
2 o'clock / up / usually / get / at / You / seven
3 ever / We / grandparents / hardly / our / visit
4 talk / I / always / my / parrot / to
5 under / My / usually / the / sleeps / cat / bed

3 Read the answers. Complete the questions.

1 *Where* does your friend live?
She lives in Seattle.
2 .... do you take your dog to the beach?
Because he loves swimming in the ocean.
3 .... do you bike to school?
Never. I don't have a bike.
4 .... is your favorite possession?
My cell phone.
5 .... is your English teacher?
My teacher is Ms. Clarkson.
6 .... do you have piano lessons?
After school on Thursdays.

4 Complete the Pet Advice sheet with *You must* or *You mustn't*.

1 *You must feed your dog twice a day.*

Pet Advice: Dogs

1	✓	feed your dog twice a day
2	✓	take your dog for a walk every day
3	✓	give your dog a place to sleep
4	✗	give your dog unhealthy food— for example, chocolate
5	✗	shout at your dog
6	✓	keep your dog on a leash

Vocabulary • Review

5 Complete these unusual animal words with *a, e, i, o* and *u.*

1 h_iss_ing c_o_ckr_oa_ch
2 t_r_nt_l_
3 pygmy g_ _t
4 g_ _nt r_bb_t
5 fr_g
6 p_r_nh_
7 pyth_n
8 p_rr_t
9 l_z_rd
10 st_ck _ns_ct

6 Look at the animals from Exercise 5 again. Find …

1 four animals with four legs. *pygmy goat, …*
2 three animals with a tail.
3 two animals with six legs.
4 two animals with no legs.
5 one animal with two legs.
6 one animal with eight legs.

7 Complete the sentences with these words.

arms	beak	fingers	neck
paws	tail	toes	~~wings~~

1 My parrot can fly because she has *wings*.
She eats her food with her .... .
2 My dog has four white .... and a black .... .
3 I have ten .... on my feet and ten .... on my hands.
4 Chimpanzees have two legs and two .... .
5 Giraffes have four long legs and a long .... .

Speaking • Review

8 Make sentences. Then listen and check.
2.10
Jim you / like / play / baseball?
Do you like playing baseball?
Mike No, I don't. I like / watch / baseball on TV. you / like / watch / TV?
Jim No. I love / listen / to music and read / books, but I hate / watch TV.

Dictation

9 Listen and write in your notebook.
2.11

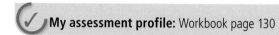

✓ **My assessment profile:** Workbook page 130

Lavindya's Profile

Age	Home country
6	India

City

Chennai

Reading

1 **Read Lavindya's profile. Are the statements true (T) or false (F)?**

1 Lavindya lives in the US.
2 She is ten years old.
3 She lives in Chennai.

2 **Read about Lavindya and her family.**
2.12 **Answer the questions.**

1 Where does Lavindya take a bath?
in a small pool outside
2 Why does she live at Arignar Anna Zoo?
3 How does she go to school?
4 What does she do in the afternoon?
5 What does she do when the elephants are tired?

Lavindya's Best Friend

It is seven o'clock in the morning in Chennai, southern India. Lavindya always takes her morning bath before school. But she doesn't take a bath at home. She takes a bath in a small pool outside with her best friend, a baby elephant!

Lavindya lives at Arignar Anna Zoo with her parents, brothers and sisters. Her father is a "mahout"—he works at the zoo, and he is a special keeper for the baby elephants. Lavindya is only six years old, but she can control the elephants, and she has a special friendship with them.

At eight o'clock in the morning, Lavindya goes to school, but she doesn't take the school bus. She rides an elephant to school. The elephant carries her backpack with its trunk. After school, Lavindya plays soccer with the elephants.

Now it is the evening, and the baby elephants are tired. Lavindya lies down next to them and pats their trunks. Sometimes they all sleep together—friends together in the day and friends together at night.

Class discussion

- Can you see elephants in your local zoo?
- How do you go to school in the morning?
- Think of three reasons why it's good to have a friendship with an animal.

5 Out and About!

Grammar
Present continuous;
Present simple and
Present continuous

Vocabulary
Activities; Weather
and seasons

Speaking
Expressing surprise

Writing
A blog

Word list page 77
Workbook page 108

Vocabulary • Activities

1 Match the photos to these words. Then listen, check and repeat.
2.13

> bowling
> climbing
> dancing
> gymnastics
> hiking
> horseback riding
> ice skating
> kayaking
> mountain biking
> painting
> playing an instrument
> rollerblading
> singing
> surfing *1*

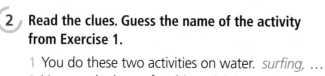

2 Read the clues. Guess the name of the activity from Exercise 1.

1 You do these two activities on water. *surfing, …*
2 You need a horse for this activity.
3 You need a bicycle for this activity.
4 You use a ball in this activity.
5 You walk a lot in this activity.
6 You make music in these two activities.

3 Listen. Copy and complete the activities Joe and
2.14 Lisa do at the Vacation Camp.

	morning	afternoon
Joe	*mountain biking*	
Lisa		

4 Write three sentences about activities you like and don't like.

I like rollerblading, but I don't like kayaking.

**Brain Trainer
Activity 3**
Go to page 116

Reading

1 Read the text quickly. Match the photos (1–4) to the correct paragraphs (A–D).

2 Read the text and check your answer to Exercise 1.

3 Read the text again. Choose the correct options.

2.15
1 Ricardo *is / isn't* at college today.
2 The first thing Ricky does is *mountain biking / climbing*.
3 The reporter, Amanda, *likes / doesn't like* hiking up Corcovado Mountain.
4 Ricky and Amanda are on Copacabana beach in the *morning / afternoon*.
5 A lot of people in Brazil *like / don't like* surfing.
6 Ricky is very good at *swimming / surfing*.

4 Guess the job. Then listen to Ricky and check.

2.16

5 What about you? In pairs, ask and answer.
1 What sports/activities are popular in your country?
2 What sports do you like?
3 What activities do you usually do in your free time?

> What sports are popular in your country?

> A lot of people like rollerblading.

Guess the Job!

Reporter Amanda Moreno is spending the day with nineteen-year-old Ricardo Dos Santos. He's a college student from Brazil.

A It's 6 a.m., and I'm having breakfast with Ricardo—nickname Ricky—on Corcovado Mountain in Rio de Janeiro. It's December, so the weather is great at the moment. The students aren't studying—they're on vacation. Today I'm taking photos of Ricky for our **Guess the job!** competition.

B Ricky's first activity today is mountain biking. He isn't riding down the street—he's riding up the street. It isn't easy!

C It's 11 a.m. Now we're hiking up the mountain for Ricky's next activities. I'm not enjoying it, but Ricky likes walking and climbing. Now we're at the top. Ricky is rollerblading and skateboarding. He's having fun!

D Now it's 4 p.m. We aren't on the mountain; we're on Copacabana beach. Ricky is swimming and surfing. Surfing is a popular sport here, and Ricky is very good at it. But why is he doing all these activities? Can you guess the job?

Is Ricky ...
a a professional sports player?
b a stuntman in a movie?
c a vacation camp counselor?
Email your answers to:
guessthejob@smart.com

Grammar • Present continuous

Affirmative	
I	'm (am) singing.
He/She/It	's (is) singing.
You/We/They	're (are) singing.

Negative	
I	'm (am) not singing.
He/She/It	isn't (is not) singing.
You/We/They	aren't (are not) singing.

Questions and short answers	
Am I singing?	Yes, I am. No, I'm not.
Is he/she/it singing?	Yes, he/she/it is. No, he/she/it isn't.
Are you/we/they singing?	Yes, you/we/they are. No, you/we/they aren't.

Grammar reference Workbook page 94

Watch Out!

run → running   write → writing
have → having

1 Study the grammar table. Choose the correct options to complete the rules.

1 The verb *to do / to be* goes before the main verb in the Present continuous.
2 We add *-ing / -es* to the end of the main verb.
3 The verb *to be* goes *before / after* the main verb in questions in the Present continuous.

2 Write the *-ing* forms of the verbs.

1 go *going*   3 do   5 swim   7 play
2 watch   4 have   6 walk   8 run

Pronunciation *-ing* endings

3a Listen to the verbs and the *-ing* endings
2.17 from Exercise 2.

b What sound does the *i* make?
2.17 Say *-ing* aloud.

c Listen again and repeat.
2.17

4 Make sentences.

1 Juan (not get up / sleep).
Juan isn't getting up. He's sleeping.
2 Enrique and Erica (not ice skate / bowl).
3 Mr. Chapman (not surf / sing).
4 Adriana and I (not study / dance).
5 I (not skateboard / paint my room).
6 Ms. Green (not swim / run).

5 Complete the text with the verbs. Use the Present
2.18 continuous. Listen and check.

The dance act you ¹ *are watching* (watch) now is the Hot Street Crew! Look at this! Kayla ² .... (not dance); she ³ .... (do) gymnastics here! Now Leroy and Des ⁴ .... (jump)! They ⁵ .... (have) fun! In the studio, the audience ⁶ .... (not sit) down. Everyone is standing and clapping. What a great dance!

6 Look at the picture and answer the questions.

It's 9 p.m. in Puebla, Mexico.

1 Is the Morales family sitting in the living room?
Yes, it is.
2 Is Elena watching TV?
3 Is her mom writing a letter?
4 Is the dog having dinner?

7 Make questions. Ask and answer for Elena.

1 your dog / sleep?
2 your parents / read?
3 you / sit / next to your mom?
4 you and your parents / eat / pizza?

8 What about you? Imagine it's 6 p.m. on Saturday. What are you doing now?

I'm listening to my favorite band on my MP3 player.

Vocabulary • Weather and seasons

1 Match the pictures to these words. Then listen, check and repeat.
2.19

autumn/fall	cloudy	cold	foggy	hot
raining *1*	snowing	spring	summer	sunny
warm	windy	winter		

Word list page 77
Workbook page 108

2 Look at the picture. Complete the sentences with the weather words from Exercise 1. Then listen, check and repeat.
2.20

What's the weather like today?

Let's look at the weather in the US. In Texas, the weather is ¹ *hot* right now.
In California, it's a nice ² .... day. But it's ³ .... in Alabama. It's ⁴ .... there, too.
Montana is very ⁵ .... , and it's ⁶ .... as well.
In Florida, they have nice ⁷ .... weather, but it's ⁸ .... , too.
And in Michigan, the weather isn't cold, but it's ⁹ .... .

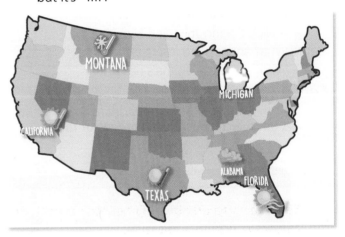

3 Listen. Choose the correct weather.
2.21

1 **a** It's raining.   **b** It's cold.   **c** It's foggy.
2 **a** It's sunny.   **b** It's snowing.   **c** It's cloudy.
3 **a** It's windy.   **b** It's cloudy.   **c** It's sunny.
4 **a** It's cold.   **b** It's warm.   **c** It's hot.

4 Look at the map in Exercise 2. In pairs, ask and answer.

Is it foggy in Montana?

No, it isn't.

**Brain Trainer
Activity 4**
Go to page 116

Chatroom Expressing surprise

Speaking and Listening

1 **Look at the photos. Which of these things can you see?**

1 a dog   4 a rat
2 a farm   5 a river
3 an otter 6 a bridge

2 **Listen and read the conversation.**
2.22 **Answer the questions.**

1 Where are the children?
They are at Willow End.
2 What does Monica often do in the summer?
3 Is Nick filming Julia and Monica?
4 What animals are in the water?
5 What are these animals doing?
6 What does Julia tell Nick to do?

3 **Act out the conversation in groups of three.**

Monica We're here! This is Willow End. It's my favorite place. It's nice in the summer—I often swim in the river here.
Julia But not today! Brrr! The water's very cold.
Nick Wow! This is an amazing place!
Monica Look at the bridge.
Julia Great! I love it!
Monica Hey! Are you filming us with your cell phone, Nick?
Nick No. I'm looking at that animal in the water.
Julia Yuck! Is it a rat?
Monica No, it's an otter. I sometimes see them here.
Nick Really? There aren't many otters. They're very rare. Look! Two otters! They're swimming.
Julia How amazing! Take a photo, Nick.

Say it in your language ...
We're here!
Yuck!

4 **Look back at the conversation. Match an expression to each object.**

1 Wow!
2 Great!
3 How amazing!

a Willow End
b the otters
c the bridge

5 **Read the phrases for expressing surprise.**

Something nice surprises you	You are surprised by some information	You are surprised by an event
Wow! Great! How amazing!	Really?	Look! Hey!

6 **Listen to the conversation. Act out the conversation in pairs.**

2.23

Stella Hi, Steve. It's me, Stella. Guess what I'm doing!
Steve I don't know. [1] Are you shopping at the mall?
Stella No. I'm [2] having coffee in the Rain Forest Café.
Steve Really?
Stella And [3] Brad Pitt is standing near me. I'm taking a photo.
Steve Wow! How amazing!

7 **Work in pairs. Replace the words in purple in Exercise 6 with these words. Act out the conversation.**

Are you going to the movies?

No. I'm bowling with my friends.

1 eating at a pizza place / sitting on a bus / going to a baseball game

2 watching a baseball game / waiting for a movie premiere / going to a concert

3 actor / singer / athlete

8 **Act out the conversation again with your own words and ideas.**

Grammar • Present simple and Present continuous

Present simple	Present continuous
I often swim here.	They're swimming.
I sometimes see them.	He's looking at the animals now.

Watch Out!

always, usually, often, sometimes, hardly ever, never → every day / week / month

happening now, at the moment

Grammar reference Workbook page 94

1 **Study the grammar table. Match the tenses to the actions.**

1 Present simple
2 Present continuous

a action happening now
b routine

2 **Do we use the Present simple or the Present continuous with these words?**

1 now *Present continuous*
2 always
3 every week
4 today

5 usually
6 never
7 at the moment

3 **Are these sentences in the Present simple (Ps) or Present continuous (Pc)?**

1 They're playing soccer at the moment. *Pc*
2 My grandma comes for dinner every Sunday.
3 Do you usually get up at 6 a.m.?
4 Jim isn't watching TV now.
5 He is studying today.
6 We get up late on Saturdays.

4 **Choose the correct options.**

1 Harry and Lucy *go / are going* on a school trip.
2 I often *do / am doing* my homework in the living room.
3 He *doesn't go / isn't going* ice skating every day.
4 *Do they climb / Are they climbing* at the moment?
5 Jenny *gets up / is getting up* late on Saturdays.
6 The dog *doesn't sleep / isn't sleeping* now.

Reading

1 Look quickly at the texts. What kind of texts do you think they are?

1 articles   2 emails   3 poems

The Fog

I like the fog,
It's soft and cool,
It hides everything,
On the way to school.

I can't see a house,
I can't see a tree,
Because the fog
Is playing with me.

The sun comes out,
The fog goes away,
But it will be back
Another day.

Anonymous

Weather

Weather is hot,
Weather is cold,
Weather is changing
As the weeks unfold.

Skies are cloudy,
Skies are fair,
Skies are changing
In the air.

It is raining,
It is snowing,
It is windy
With breezes blowing.

Days are foggy,
Days are clear,
Weather is changing
Throughout the year!

Meish Goldish

Autumn wind
The mountain's shadow
is trembling

Kobayashi Issa

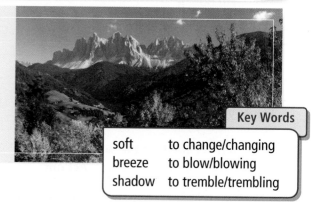

Key Words

soft	to change/changing
breeze	to blow/blowing
shadow	to tremble/trembling

2 Read and check your answer to Exercise 1.

3 Read this definition of a haiku. Which poem is a haiku?

A haiku is a very short Japanese poem. A haiku usually talks about one of the four seasons.

4 Read the poems again. Answer the questions.
2.24
1 Does "The Fog" poet like fog? *Yes, he does.*
2 Is the "Weather" poem talking about weather at one time of year?
3 Which season is the haiku about?
4 Which poem has four stanzas?
5 Which poem doesn't use rhyme?
6 How many weather words can you find in all the poems?

Listening

1 Listen and match the people (1–3) to the season
2.25 they are talking about.

1 Blake   a spring
2 Yoko   b summer
3 Paolo   c fall

2 Listen again. Are the statements true (T)
2.25 or false (F)?

1 Blake is from Canada.
2 Blake likes the color of autumn flowers.
3 Yoko is American.
4 Cherry blossoms are pink and white.
5 Paolo likes summer.
6 Summer in Argentina is in July.

Writing • A blog

1 **Read the Writing File.**

> **Writing File**   Word order
>
> The subject of a sentence comes before
> the verb in English.
> *I get up at 6 a.m.*
> *Sam and Anna are having breakfast.*

2 **Read Julio's blog. Find the verbs that follow
these subjects.**

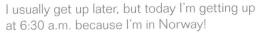

    1 I   2 he/Erik   3 we

Monday Morning

I usually get up later, but today I'm getting up
at 6:30 a.m. because I'm in Norway!

We're on a school exchange trip to Tromsø,
a city in the Arctic Circle. It's really cold here!
It's snowing now, and it's foggy, too. In winter
there are usually only a couple of hours of light
in the day.

Erik is my exchange buddy. He lives here,
and he loves winter sports. He often goes
kayaking and ice skating. Do you know that
Tromsø is Norway's candidate for the 2018
Winter Olympics?

It's 7 a.m. now, and Erik is waiting for me
with snowshoes. We use them to go
to school—it's cool!

Julio

3 **Put the words in the correct order
to make sentences.**

  1 writing / her blog / is / Layla
    Layla is writing her blog.
  2 go to school / We / at eight thirty
  3 The dog / swimming / in the river / is
  4 like / rollerblading / They
  5 Nat and Mia / are / in the mountains / hiking

4 **Read the blog again. Answer the questions.**

  1 Why is Julio in Norway?
    Because he is on a school exchange trip.
  2 What is the weather like in Tromsø?
  3 Is it light all day in Tromsø in winter?
  4 What activities does Erik like?
  5 What is Erik doing now?

5 **Imagine you are on an exchange trip. Answer
the questions about your trip.**

  1 What time do you usually get up?
  2 Are you doing things at different times today?
  3 Where are you?
  4 What is the weather like in this place?
  5 What is the weather like at home?
  6 Who is your exchange buddy?
  7 What activities does he/she like?

6 **Write a short blog about your exchange trip. Use
"My blog" and your answers from Exercise 5.**

> **My blog**
>
> **Paragraph 1**   introducing a topic
> *I usually … , but today I … .*
> **Paragraph 2**   talking about a place
> *It's … in … . (place)*
> **Paragraph 3**   talking about a person
> *(name) is … .*
> *He/She lives / likes / often goes … .*

Remember!
- Check word order for subjects and verbs.
- Use the vocabulary in this unit.
- Check your grammar, spelling
  and punctuation.

Refresh Your Memory!

Grammar • Review

1 Complete the postcard with the verbs in the Present continuous.

Hi Tania,

We ¹ 're enjoying (enjoy) our family vacation in Tampa. I ² .... (sit) by the swimming pool with my little brother, Jack. I ³ .... (watch) him because my parents ⁴ .... (make) dinner.

Jack ⁵ .... (not swim) at the moment. He ⁶ .... (play) with some cats. The cats ⁷ .... (run) away from my brother—they ⁸ .... (not have) fun!

See you soon,

Nicole

Tania Bexon
34 Hancock St
Dover, NH 03820

2 Make questions with the Present continuous.

1 you / sit / in a classroom?
   Are you sitting in a classroom?
2 your teacher / talk / to the class?
3 you / watch / TV?
4 you and your friend / talk?
5 all the students / listen / to the teacher?
6 your friend / write / in his/her notebook?

3 Answer the questions in Exercise 2.

1 *Yes, I am.*

4 Put the verbs in the Present simple or the Present continuous.

1 Georgia (brush) her teeth every morning.
   Georgia brushes her teeth every morning.
2 We (have) our breakfast now.
3 It (not rain) at the moment.
4 He often (hike) in the spring.
5 They (rollerblade) in the park now.
6 She never (watch) TV after 10 p.m.
7 He (study) every day.
8 I (visit) my grandma today.

Vocabulary • Review

5 Find the one that doesn't fit.

1 **a** kayaking
  b *horseback riding*
  c surfing
2 **a** ice skating
  b singing
  c dancing
3 **a** climbing
  b hiking
  c playing an instrument
4 **a** rollerblading
  b bowling
  c painting
5 **a** singing
  b horseback riding
  c hiking

6 Complete the sentences with a weather word.

1 It isn't sunny today. It's r*aining*.
2 It's warm today, but it's c _ _ _ _ _, too.
3 It's very cold today, and it's s _ _ _ _ _ _ now.
4 The weather is w _ _ _ _ and cold today.
5 This morning it's very gray and f _ _ _ _ outside.

Speaking • Review

7 Choose the correct option to complete each
2.26 conversation. Then listen and check.

1
Girl *Hey! / Wow!* What are you doing?
Boy I'm taking a photo of you! Smile!

2
Girl Guess what! I have tickets for the Kings of Leon concert tonight!
Boy *Look! / Really?*

3
Boy Jennifer Lopez is sitting near me.
Girl *How amazing! / Hey!*

Dictation

8 Listen and write in your notebook.
2.27

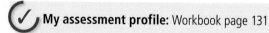

✓ **My assessment profile:** Workbook page 131

Science File

Why Is the Sky Blue?

This experiment shows us why the sky is blue.

You need ...

- a flashlight
- a 1-liter plastic bottle
- some milk
- some water

---

1 Put 750 ml of water into the bottle.

2 Put the flashlight under the bottle and turn it on. Look down on it from above. What color is the light?

3 Add one teaspoon of milk to the water and mix it together. Shine the flashlight again and look down on the bottle. Now the light in the middle of the bottle is orange, and the light at the sides of the bottle is blue.

Why does this happen?

The light from the flashlight has a lot of different colors. When it passes through the milk and water mixture, it breaks up into different-colored light waves. The blue light wave is short. The orange light wave is long. So the blue light wave is at the side of the bottle, and the orange light wave is at the top of the bottle.

In the same way, light from the sun breaks up into different colors when it comes into our atmosphere. In the day, we see the short blue light waves. At sunset and at sunrise, we see the long red and orange light waves.

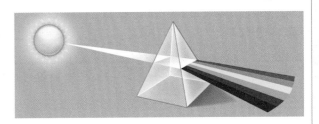

Reading

1 Read the text quickly. Match 1–2 to a–b.

1 Blue light waves are ...   a long.
2 Orange light waves are ...   b short.

2 Read the text again. Answer the questions.

2.28

1 What color is the light in the middle of the bottle? *orange*
2 What color is the light at the sides of the bottle?
3 What happens when the light passes through the water and milk mixture?
4 What happens when light from the sun comes into our atmosphere?

My Science File

3 Find out about rainbows. Find out ...

- when rainbows happen.
- why we see rainbows.

4 In pairs, create an experiment to make a rainbow. Use some of these things:

- a flashlight
- a glass
- a bottle of water
- a sheet of paper
- a mirror
- a CD or DVD
- a window

5 Write your instructions for the experiment in your notebook.

Delicious!

Grammar
Countable and uncountable nouns;
Many/Much/A lot of;
Comparatives

Vocabulary
Food and drinks;
Adjectives

Speaking
Ordering food

Writing
Instructions

Word list page 77
Workbook page 109

Vocabulary • Food and drinks

1 Match the pictures (1–16) to these words. Then listen, check and repeat.

2.29

banana	bread	broccoli	cheese	chicken	eggs
ham	juice	pasta	rice	salmon	sausage
shrimp	tea	tomatoes	tuna	water	yogurt *1*

2 Copy and complete the table with food from Exercise 1.

Carbohydrates	Fish
bread, ...	*tuna, ...*
Fruits and Vegetables	**Dairy**
banana, ...	*cheese, ...*
Meat	**Drinks**
sausage, ...	*water, ...*

3 In pairs, ask and answer.

1 What do you usually have for breakfast/ lunch/dinner?
2 What's your favorite food?
3 What's your favorite drink?

> What do you usually have for breakfast?

> I usually have bread and cheese.

**Brain Trainer
Activity 3**
Go to page 117

Reading

1 **Look at the photos. Write *Juanita*, *Caitlin* or *Chuck*.**

1 This person's refrigerator has some fruits in it.
2 This person's refrigerator has 24 eggs in it.
3 This person's refrigerator has 10 carrots in it.

2 **Read and check your answers to Exercise 1.**

3 **Read the article again. Are the statements**
2.30 **true (T) or false (F)?**

1 Juanita doesn't have any fish in her fridge. *F*
2 Juanita likes rice salad.
3 Caitlin likes meat.
4 Caitlin's family doesn't drink much water.
5 There is a lot of sausage in Chuck's fridge.
6 Chuck doesn't like yogurt.

4 **What about you? In pairs, ask and answer.**

1 What's in your fridge at home?
2 Are you a vegetarian?
3 Are you a good cook?
4 What food don't you like?

What's in your fridge at home?

I think we have some vegetables, cheese, …

Look!
This Is Our Refrigerator!

Juanita

I live in El Calafate, a small town in Patagonia. Today we're preparing a barbecue, so we have a lot of chicken, sausage and salmon in our fridge. There's a rice salad with shrimp and tuna—it's delicious! We also have twenty-four eggs because my mom loves making cakes.

Caitlin

My family is from Scotland, and we're vegetarians, so we don't have any meat in our fridge. We usually have a lot of vegetables, and today we have some broccoli, ten carrots and a lot of tomatoes. We don't have any milk, and we don't have much juice, but that's OK because we all drink a lot of water.

Chuck

We're from Wisconsin. I have a big family and a very big fridge! Today we have some ham, a lot of bread and sausage. We don't have many eggs, but there's a lot of yogurt because we all love yogurt. We also have a lot of fruit because I often make smoothies for breakfast.

Grammar

● Countable and uncountable nouns

Countable nouns		Uncountable nouns
Singular	Plural	
a banana	some bananas	some bread
an apple	some apples	some rice
an egg	some eggs	some pasta

1 Study the grammar table. Choose the correct options to complete the rule.

> We use *much* / *many* with countable nouns and *much* / *many* with uncountable nouns.

2 Are these words countable or uncountable?

1 chicken *uncountable*
2 broccoli
3 vegetable
4 water
5 tomato

6 sausage
7 banana
8 salmon
9 tuna
10 yogurt

Pronunciation Word stress

3a Listen to the words in Exercise 2.
2.31 Where is the stress?

*chi*cken

b Listen again. Copy and put the words
2.31 under the correct heading.

chicken	to**ma**to

c Listen again and repeat.
2.31

● Many/Much/A lot of

How many?	How much?
How many eggs do you have?	How much bread do you have?
We don't have any eggs.	We don't have any bread.
We don't have many eggs.	We don't have much bread.
We have some/four eggs.	We have some bread.
We have a lot of eggs.	We have a lot of bread.

Grammar reference Workbook page 96

4 Look at the picture. Choose the correct options.

1 How *much* / *many* pasta is on the table?
2 How *much* / *many* eggs are on the table?
3 How *much* / *many* bread is on the table?
4 How *much* / *many* cheese is on the table?
5 How *much* / *many* tomatoes are on the table?

5 Answer the questions in Exercise 4.
Use *not much/many* or *a lot of*.

1 *There is a lot of pasta.*

6 Complete the conversation with these words.

Not much   much   many   ~~some~~   a lot of

Chen What's in your lunch box, Billy?
Billy I have ¹*some* ham sandwiches.
Chen How ² .... sandwiches do you have?
Billy Four.
Chen That's ³ .... sandwiches! And how
⁴ .... water do you have?
Billy ⁵ .... . My water bottle is very small.

7 What about you? What's in your favorite sandwich? In pairs, ask and answer.

> What do you have in your sandwich?

> I have a lot of chicken and some tomatoes.

Vocabulary • Adjectives

1 **Look at the pictures and choose the correct options to complete the sentences. Then listen, check and repeat.**
2.32

clean	cold	delicious	dirty	disgusting	horrible
hot	large	noisy	quiet	small	~~wonderful~~

Word list page 77
Workbook page 109

1 Fernando's is a *wonderful* / *horrible* restaurant!
2 The coffee is *hot* / *cold*.
3 The food is *disgusting* / *delicious*!
4 We have *small* / *large* tables.
5 The music is *quiet* / *noisy*.
6 The kitchen is very *clean* / *dirty*.

7 Fernando's is a *wonderful* / *horrible* restaurant!
8 The coffee is *hot* / *cold*.
9 The food is *disgusting* / *delicious*!
10 We have *small* / *large* tables.
11 The music is *quiet* / *noisy*.
12 The kitchen is very *clean* / *dirty*.

2 **Say the opposites.**

1 quiet *noisy*
2 small
3 clean
4 hot
5 delicious
6 horrible

3 **Choose the correct options.**

1 Don't eat this food! It's *clean* / *delicious* / *disgusting*.
2 I can't hear the radio. It's very *small* / *cold* / *quiet*.
3 I don't want this tea. It's *large* / *noisy* / *cold*.
4 There are 2,000 students in this school. It's a *quiet* / *large* / *delicious* school.
5 I like this book. It's *horrible* / *wonderful* / *quiet*.
6 Don't sit there. The table is *noisy* / *dirty* / *wonderful*.

4 **Complete the text with these words. Then listen and check.**
2.33

clean	delicious	large
quiet	~~small~~	wonderful

I love visiting my aunt. She lives in a ¹ *small* house in the country with only two rooms, but the yard is ² ....—it's almost 30 meters long! It's always ³ .... at my aunt's house because there aren't any cars or people near her. My aunt hates dirt, so her house is always very ⁴ .... . My favorite time of day at my aunt's house is dessert. My aunt is a ⁵ .... cook, and she makes ⁶ .... cakes. I love eating them!

Brain Trainer
Activity 4
Go to page 117

Speaking and Listening

1 Look at the photo. Answer the question.

1 Where are Monica, Julia, Nick and Leo?

2 Listen and read the conversation.
2.34 Answer the questions.

1 Why are the children at the restaurant?
It's Nick's birthday.

2 Do they sit at the small table
or the large table?

3 What does Julia order?

4 Who orders the pasta with chicken?

5 Who orders some garlic bread?

6 Who doesn't want a drink?

7 Does Monica like her pizza?

3 Act out the conversation in groups of five.

Julia	Hi, everyone! Happy birthday, Nick! Is this table OK?
Nick	It's very small. That table's better. It's larger.
Monica	Yes, but it's much noisier. Let's stay here.
Julia	OK. Here's the menu.
Waiter	Are you ready to order?
Julia	Yes. I'd like the ham and cheese pizza, please.
Monica	Me too!
Nick	I'll have the pasta with chicken, please. And some garlic bread. Yum!
Leo	Spaghetti with tomato sauce for me, please.
Waiter	And would you like anything to drink?
Monica	No, I'm OK, thanks.
Nick	Can we have some water, please?
Waiter	Yes, of course.
	***
Waiter	How is your food?
Monica	It's delicious, thanks.

Say it in your language ...

Yum!

Yes, of course.

4 **Look back at the conversation. What questions does the waiter ask? How do the children reply?**

Waiter … *Are you ready to order?*

Children …

5 **Read the phrases for ordering food in a restaurant.**

Waiter	Customer
Are you ready to order? Would you like anything to drink? Yes, of course. How is your food?	I'd like the ham and cheese pizza, please. I'll have the pasta with chicken, please. Spaghetti with tomato sauce for me, please. No, I'm OK, thanks. Can we have some water, please? It's delicious, thanks.

6 **Listen to the conversation. Act out the**
2.35 **conversation in groups of four.**

Waiter Are you ready to order?
Nick Yes. I'll have the [1] cheese sandwich, please.
Monica I'd like the [2] salmon with broccoli, please.
Julia I'll have the [3] tuna salad, please.
Waiter Would you like anything to drink?
Nick No, I'm OK, thanks.
Monica Me too!
Julia Can I have a glass of [4] orange juice, please?
Waiter Yes, of course.

7 **Work in groups of four. Replace the words in purple in Exercise 6. Use these words and/or your own ideas. Act out the conversations.**

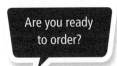
Are you ready to order?

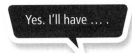
Yes. I'll have … .

1 ham sandwich / chicken sandwich / egg sandwich

2 sausage with carrots / tuna with tomatoes / pasta with shrimp

3 egg salad / ham salad / tuna salad

4 apple juice / water

Grammar • Comparatives

Short adjectives	
small	smaller
clean	cleaner
hot	hotter

Short adjectives ending in **-e**	
large	larger

Adjectives ending in **-y**	
dirty	dirtier

Long adjectives	
wonderful	more wonderful

Irregular adjectives	
bad	worse
good	better

Watch Out!
Her school is smaller than your school.
The pasta is more delicious than the pizza.

Grammar reference Workbook page 96

1 **Study the grammar table. Complete the rules.**

To make the comparative form, we add [1] …. to the end of a short adjective, and use the word [2] …. in front of a long adjective.

2 **Complete the sentences with the comparative adjectives.**

1 My house is *colder (cold)* than your house.
2 This table is …. *(noisy)* than that table.
3 The chicken is …. *(delicious)* than the fish.
4 The poster is …. *(cheap)* than the DVD.
5 My watch is …. *(new)* than your watch.
6 Harry's camera is …. *(expensive)* than Sam's camera.

3 **Work in pairs. Find five differences between you and your partner. Use these ideas.**

1 old / young
2 long / short hair
3 large / small family
4 light / dark eyes
5 big backpack / small backpack

Reading

1 Look at the photos. What are the places?
  a vacation camps
  b restaurants
  c hotels

Three Unusual ...

Every week we find three unusual places around the world. This week we're looking at amazing restaurants from three different countries.

Ithaa: The Undersea Restaurant

You can watch the fish and listen to the ocean in this restaurant. It's in the Maldives, and it's five meters below sea level. There is space for fourteen people in the restaurant. The food is expensive—dinner for two people is $150—but the view is wonderful.

The Treehouse Restaurant

Do you like being outside? Do you like looking at the trees and the sky? This restaurant is ten meters above the ground in a treehouse in a forest in New Zealand. You can have lunch or dinner, look at the trees and listen to the birds. Bring a sweater because it's cold here in the evenings.

Dinner in the Sky

The home of this restaurant is Belgium, but it can be in New York, London, Paris ... or in your hometown! It travels around the world on a big trailer. Do you want a view of a city or of the ocean? You can choose with "Dinner in the Sky." There is one large table with 22 chairs, and it is 50 meters above the ground! Don't look down!

Key Words		
unusual	below	space
outside	sweater	trailer

2 Read the text and check your answer to Exercise 1.

3 Read the text again. Answer the questions.

2.36
  1 Is Ithaa a cheap restaurant?
    No, it's an expensive restaurant.
  2 How many people can eat at Ithaa?
  3 Why do you need warm clothes for the Treehouse Restaurant?
  4 What animals can you listen to at the Treehouse Restaurant?
  5 How many people can eat at Dinner in the Sky?
  6 What's special about Dinner in the Sky?

Listening

1 Match the national dishes (1–3) to the countries (a–c).

  1 empanada   a England
  2 moussaka   b Chile
  3 fish and chips   c Greece

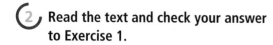

2 Listen and check your answers to Exercise 1.
2.37

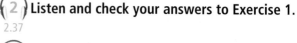

3 Listen again. Are the statements true (T)
2.37 or false (F)?

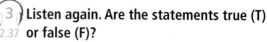

  1 Diego is from Greece.
  2 An empanada has meat or vegetables inside.
  3 There is fish and cheese in moussaka.
  4 A lot of people in England like fish and chips.

Writing • Instructions

1 **Read the Writing File.**

> **Writing File** Sequence words
>
> First, open the bag.
> Then take out the chips.
> Finally, eat the chips.

2 **Read the recipe. Find the sequence words**
first, then **and** *finally.*

Chop! Add! Pour!

Banana and Raspberry Yogurt Smoothie

Blend!

Ingredients
- 1 banana
- 10–12 raspberries
- 5 tablespoons of raspberry yogurt
- 3 tablespoons of milk

First, chop the banana. Put the banana into a blender. Then add the raspberries, the yogurt and the milk. Blend for thirty seconds. Finally, pour the mixture into a glass and drink it! You can add sugar, but it's better without sugar.

You can also make frozen smoothies with this recipe. First, pour the drink into small paper cups. Then put a stick into each cup and put the cups in the freezer. Finally, wait two hours and then take a cup out of the freezer. Enjoy your frozen yogurt smoothie!

Smoothie

3 **Put these sentences into the correct order. Rewrite them using** *first, then* **and** *finally.*

How to make a cup of tea:
a add hot water.
b drink your tea.
c put the teabag into the cup.

4 **Read the recipe again. Answer the questions.**

1 How many bananas do you need? *one*
2 How much yogurt do you need?
3 Is the recipe better with some sugar?
4 Where do you put the paper cups?

5 **Create your own milkshake recipe. Choose two or three ingredients from the list below.**

ice cream
banana
raspberry
strawberry
mango
pineapple
cocoa

6 **Write your recipe. Use "My milkshake" and your ingredients from Exercise 5.**

> **My milkshake** ⊗
>
> .... and .... Milkshake
> Ingredients
> - 250 ml of milk
> - 1 / 2 / 3 …
> - 2 / 3 tablespoons of …
>
> First, … . / Then … . / Finally, … .
> You can also make … .
> Enjoy your … .

Remember!
- Use sequence words (*first, then, finally*).
- Use the vocabulary in this unit.
- Check your grammar, spelling and punctuation.

Grammar • Review

1 Are these words countable (C) or uncountable (U)?

banana C	broccoli	cheese	egg
ham	pasta	rice	sausage
shrimp	tomatoes	water	yogurt

2 Choose the correct options to complete the conversation.

Joe How *much* / *many* chicken do we have in the fridge?

Freda Not *much* / *many*.

Joe Oh, OK. What about eggs, and bread?

Freda We have *much* / *a lot of* eggs, but we don't have *much* / *many* bread.

Joe How *much* / *many* sausage do we have?

Freda We have half a kilo of sausage, but we don't have *any* / *no* ham.

Joe How *much* / *many* cheese do we have?

Freda We have *a lot of* / *much* cheese.

3 Make the comparative form of these adjectives.

1 delicious *more delicious*
2 large
3 dirty
4 small
5 cold
6 noisy
7 wonderful
8 clean

4 Make sentences with comparative adjectives.

1 Lucy's cell phone / small / Sally's cell phone
Lucy's cell phone is smaller than Sally's cell phone.
2 My bike / large / your scooter
3 The summer in California / hot / in Rhode Island
4 The Italian restaurant / good / the Chinese restaurant
5 My bedroom / clean / your bedroom
6 Your dog / noisy / my dog
7 Towns / quiet / cities
8 The pizza / delicious / the pasta

Vocabulary • Review

5 Complete the food words.

1 c *h e e s e*
2 t _ _ a _ _ _ s
3 b r _ _ _ _ _ i
4 j _ i _ _
5 _ r _ _ d

6 Complete the sentences with these words.

clean	~~delicious~~	disgusting	large
quiet	small	wonderful	

1 This egg sandwich is *delicious*, but it's very ..... I want another sandwich now!
2 You must have .... hands when you cook food.
3 My MP3 player's very .... ! I can't hear the music.
4 This yogurt is old. It's .... .
5 I love this movie. It's .... !
6 My cousin lives in a very .... house. It has six bedrooms and four bathrooms.

Speaking • Review

7 Put these phrases into the correct place in the conversation. Then listen and check. *2.38*

I'll have	It's delicious	~~Are you ready to order?~~
I'm OK	Would you like	

Waiter ¹ *Are you ready to order?*
Greg Yes. I'd like the pasta with tomatoes, please.
Bea ² .... the chicken with broccoli, please.
Waiter ³ .... anything to drink?
Greg Yes, please. Can I have a glass of water?
Bea ⁴ .... , thanks.
Waiter How is your food?
Greg ⁵ .... , thank you.

Dictation

8 Listen and write in your notebook. *2.39*

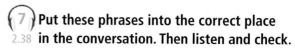
My assessment profile: Workbook page 132

Amy Singh's Profile

 Age
22

Home country
United States

City
New York City

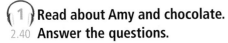

Amy and Chocolate

Early 2002

Amy Singh is nine years old. Her fourth-grade teacher asks students to do a project about anything they want to study, and Amy decides to make chocolate at home. She visits the New York City Botanical Garden to see her first cacao tree.

Late 2002

Amy contacts Maricel Presilla, an author of a book about chocolate. Maricel meets with Amy and gives her a bag of cacao beans. Different chocolate companies tell Amy that you can only make chocolate in a factory. Amy creates machines from household objects to make chocolate in her kitchen. Maricel and other experts taste Amy's chocolate and say it's delicious!

2003

It's 2003, and Amy is 10 years old. She is invited to the New York Chocolate Show, where she gives a presentation about making chocolate at home.

2007

Amy is 15 years old. She learns about a serious problem in the chocolate industry: child labor. She makes a video about children working on cacao plantations. Her video is posted on the website of the International Labor Rights Fund.

May 2013

Amy is 21 and is invited to Prague, Czech Republic, to give a talk about her chocolate story. Amy's message is "Pursue your curiosity." And when there are problems, find your "little child's voice" and "let it inspire you."

Reading

1 **Read about Amy and chocolate. Answer the questions.**
2.40

1 Why does Amy visit the Botanical Garden in 2002?
   She wants to see a cacao tree.
2 What does Maricel Presilla give Amy in 2002?
3 Where does Amy make chocolate?
4 How does Amy's chocolate taste?
5 When does Amy make a speech at the New York Chocolate Show?
6 What does Amy do in 2007?
7 What is Amy's message?

Class discussion

- Imagine you can do a school project about anything you want, just like Amy. What is your project about? Why?
- Can you cook something? What?
- Why do you think Amy is successful? What can we learn from her story?

Grammar • Adverbs of frequency

1 Make sentences about the people in the table with these adverbs.

Ella always gets up before 7 a.m.

~~always~~	hardly ever	never
often	sometimes	usually

I get up before 7 a.m.	Ella	Mia + Jade	Tom	Zak	Ali	Jo
Number of days in a year	365	2	70	150	0	351

2 Make sentences.

1 go home / They / at three thirty / usually
   They usually go home at three thirty.
2 often / is / late / She
3 hardly / eat pasta / I / ever
4 We / watch a DVD / on Fridays / always
5 at the café / are / sometimes / They / at 4:15
6 He / uses / his MP3 player / never

• Present simple with *Wh* questions

3 Make *Wh* questions for the answers with these words.

How often	What	~~When~~	Where	Who	Why

1 you / play tennis / ?
   At 4:30.
   When do you play tennis?
2 your grandparents / live / ?
   In Florida.
3 your favorite movie / ?
   Star Wars.
4 he / have PE classes / ?
   Every day.
5 Tom Cruise / ?
   He's an actor.
6 you / like / science / ?
   Because it's interesting.

• Must/Mustn't

4 Make sentences with *must* or *mustn't*.

1 they / have / breakfast / before 8 a.m.
   They must have breakfast before 8 a.m.
2 he / not / watch / TV / today
3 I / do / my math homework
4 she / brush / her teeth / every day
5 we / not / be / late for class

• Present continuous

5 Complete the sentences with the Present continuous of the verbs.

1 He *'s singing* (sing) his favorite song.
2 We .... (have) lunch at the moment.
3 They .... (not clean up) their bedroom.
4 She .... (run) to school because she's late.
5 You .... (not watch) TV.

6 Make questions and answers with the Present continuous.

1 they / use / the computer / ?   ✗
   Are they using the computer? No, they aren't.
2 it / snow / at the moment / ?   ✓
3 I / do / the correct exercise / ?   ✓
4 you / bike / a long way / ?   ✗
5 they / swim / in the ocean / ?   ✗

• Present simple and Present continuous

7 Complete the conversation with the Present simple or Present continuous.

Luke Hi, Leah. What [1] *are you doing* (you / do) at the train station?

Leah I [2] .... (wait) for my friend Susan. She [3] .... (come) here for a week.

Luke That's great!

Leah Yes. I [4] .... (hardly ever / see) her because she [5] .... (swim) in competitions every weekend. What about you? Where [6] .... (you / go) now?

Luke To the beach.

Leah But it [7] .... (rain) today!

Luke I [8] .... (always / go) to the beach in the rain.

• Countable and uncountable nouns

8 **Are these words countable (C) or uncountable (U)?**

1 broccoli *U*
2 egg
3 sausage
4 water

5 rice
6 banana
7 tea
8 shrimp

9 **Choose the correct options.**

1 How *much* / *many* water do you have?
2 I'm eating *an* / *some* egg.
3 There isn't *much* / *many* juice in the fridge.
4 We have *a* / *some* bread.
5 Is there *much* / *many* shrimp in your pasta?

10 **Complete the conversation with these words.**

a	How many	How much	lot of
many	much	some (x2)	

A Let's make ¹*a* pizza!
B ² .... cheese do we have?
A We have a ³ .... cheese. We have ⁴ .... broccoli, too. We have ⁵ .... ham, but we don't have very ⁶ .... .
B ⁷ .... tomatoes do we have? I love pizzas with tomato sauce!
A We don't have ⁸ .... tomatoes. Just a few.
B OK. Let's put them on the pizza, too. Yum!

• Comparatives

11 **Write the comparative form of the adjectives.**

1 cold *colder*
2 large
3 disgusting
4 noisy
5 bad

6 clean
7 dirty
8 good
9 hot
10 horrible

12 **Make sentences with the comparative form of the adjective.**

1 your bag: 2012 / her bag: 2013 (new)
Her bag is newer than your bag.
2 my math grade: C / my history grade: A (good)
3 Chicago: 5°C / Miami: 25°C (cold)
4 his parents: 50 / your parents: 39 (old)
5 surfing: $15 / horseback riding: $30 (expensive)

Speaking • Expressing likes and dislikes

1 **Make sentences.**

1 I / like / play / tennis
I like playing tennis.
2 I / love / swim
3 my sister / love / ice skate
4 I / not like / do / sports
5 I / hate / be / in the water

2 **Complete the conversation with the sentences from Exercise 1.**

A ¹*I love swimming.*
B I don't. ² .... .
A What's your favorite sport?
B Well, tennis is fun. ³ .... with my sister in the summer. ⁴ .... with her friends in the winter, but I never go with them. ⁵ .... when it's cold.

• Expressing surprise

3 **Complete the words.**

1 **A** I got an email from Tammi. She's in Istanbul.
  B W *o w* !
2 **A** I _ove tarantulas.
  B R _ _ _ _ y?
3 **A** I have a ticket to the Olympic Games.
  B H _ w a _ _ z _ _ _!
4 **A** L _ _ k! That movie with Ashton Kutcher is on TV.
  B Gr _ _ _! He's my favorite actor.

• Ordering food

4 **Put the conversation in the correct order.**

Customer 1	Can I have a glass of apple juice, please?	....
Waiter	Are you ready to order?	.1.
Customer 1	Yes. I'd like the salmon and rice, please. What about you, Phil?	....
Waiter	Would you like anything to drink?	....
Customer 2	Me too!	....
Customer 1	It's delicious, thank you.	....
Waiter	How is your food?	....
Customer 2	I'll have the tuna salad, please.	....

Vocabulary • Unusual animals

1 Fill in the missing letters in the words.

1 p y g <u>m y</u> g <u>o</u> a t
2 t _ r _ n t _ _ a
3 p y _ _ o n
4 p i _ _ n _ a
5 h i _ _ i n g c _ _ k r _ _ c h
6 p _ _ r _ t
7 s _ _ c k i _ s _ _ t
8 f _ _ g
9 g i _ _ t r _ _ b _ t
10 l _ z _ _ d

• Parts of the body

2 Complete the sentences with these words.

arms	beak	fingers	foot	~~head~~	legs
neck	paw	tail	toes	wings	

1 A python has a small *head* and a long body.
2 A dog has four .... , but a stick insect has six.
3 A cat has a long .... .
4 A giraffe has a long .... .
5 We have ten .... and ten .... .
6 At the end of my leg is my .... .
7 At the end of our .... , we have hands.
8 A .... is the name for a dog's foot.
9 A parrot flies with its .... and eats with its .... .

• Activities

3 Match the descriptions to these words.

climbing	hiking
~~kayaking~~	mountain biking
painting	playing an instrument
horseback riding	singing
~~surfing~~	

1 You do this on water. *kayaking, surfing*
2 You do this at a music lesson.
3 You do this in art class.
4 You can do this in a tree.
5 You ride something in this activity.
6 You walk a long way in this activity.

• Weather and seasons

4 Read Meiko's diary. Complete the words.

• **January 10**
I love [1] win <u>t e r</u> in Japan. It's very [2] c _ _ _.
Today it's [3] s _ _ _ ing. I can go skiing soon!

• **April 7**
In [4] sp _ _ _ _ we admire the pink flowers on the cherry trees. It's [5] w _ _ m outside.

• **June 15**
It's [6] r _ _ n _ _ _ today. I don't like this weather!

• **July 27**
[7] S _ _ _ er is here! It's very [8] h _ _ and [9] su _ _ _.

• **October 2**
It's [10] au _ _ _ _. There are red leaves on the trees. It's [11] cl _ _ d _ and [12] f _ _ _ y today. It's very [13] w _ _ d _, too.

• Food and drinks

5 Put the words in the correct categories.

bananas	bread	broccoli	~~cheese~~
chicken	eggs	ham	juice
pasta	rice	salmon	sausage
shrimp	tea	tomatoes	tuna
water	yogurt		

1 Dairy *cheese*
2 Fish
3 Meat
4 Fruits and Vegetables
5 Drinks
6 Carbohydrates

• Adjectives

6 Complete the sentences with these words.

clean	~~delicious~~	dirty	disgusting
large	noisy	quiet	wonderful

1 I love this food. It's *delicious*.
2 Giant rabbits are very .... .
3 Be .... . Your brother's sleeping.
4 I hate cockroaches. They're .... .
5 I'm nice and .... after my shower.
6 I'm always .... after playing soccer.
7 That parrot talks a lot. It's very .... .
8 We're having a .... vacation. I love it here!

Word list

Unit 4 • Animal Magic

Unusual animals

frog	/frɔg/
giant rabbit	/ˈdʒaɪənt ˈræbɪt/
hissing cockroach	/ˈhɪsɪŋ ˈkak-routʃ/
lizard	/ˈlɪzəd/
parrot	/ˈpærət/
piranha	/pɪˈranə/
pygmy goat	/ˈpɪgmi ˈgout/
python	/ˈpaɪθɑn/
stick insect	/ˈstɪk ˈɪnsɛkt/
tarantula	/təˈræntʃələ/

Parts of the body

arm	/ɑrm/
beak	/bik/
fin	/fɪn/
finger	/ˈfɪŋgə/
foot	/fʊt/
hand	/hænd/
head	/hɛd/
leg	/lɛg/
neck	/nɛk/
paw	/pɔ/
tail	/teɪl/
toe	/tou/
wing	/wɪŋ/

Unit 5 • Out and About!

Activities

bowling	/ˈboulɪŋ/
climbing	/ˈklaɪmɪŋ/
dancing	/ˈdænsɪŋ/
gymnastics	/dʒɪmˈnæstɪks/
hiking	/ˈhaɪkɪŋ/
horseback riding	/ˈhɔrsbæk ˈraɪdɪŋ/
ice skating	/ˈaɪs ˈskeɪtɪŋ/
kayaking	/ˈkaɪækɪŋ/
mountain biking	/ˈmaʊntˈn ˈbaɪkɪŋ/
painting	/ˈpeɪntɪŋ/
playing an instrument	/ˈpleɪɪŋ ən ˈɪnstrəmənt/
rollerblading	/ˈroulə͵bleɪdɪŋ/
singing	/ˈsɪŋɪŋ/
surfing	/ˈsəfɪŋ/

Weather and seasons

autumn/fall	/ˈɔt̬əm/, /fɔl/
cloudy	/ˈklaʊdi/
cold	/kould/
foggy	/ˈfagi/
hot	/hat/
raining	/ˈreɪnɪŋ/
snowing	/ˈsnouɪŋ/
spring	/sprɪŋ/
summer	/ˈsʌmə/
sunny	/ˈsʌni/
warm	/wɔrm/
windy	/ˈwɪndi/
winter	/ˈwɪntə/

Unit 6 • Delicious!

Food and drinks

banana	/bəˈnænə/
bread	/brɛd/
broccoli	/ˈbrakəli/
cheese	/tʃiz/
chicken	/ˈtʃɪkən/
eggs	/ɛgz/
ham	/hæm/
juice	/dʒus/
pasta	/ˈpastə/
rice	/raɪs/
salmon	/ˈsæmən/
sausage	/ˈsɔsɪdʒ/
shrimp	/ʃrɪmp/
tea	/ti/
tomatoes	/təˈmeɪtouz/
tuna	/ˈtunə/
water	/ˈwɔt̬ə/
yogurt	/ˈyougət/

Adjectives

clean	/klin/
cold	/kould/
delicious	/dɪˈlɪʃəs/
dirty	/ˈdəti/
disgusting	/dɪsˈgʌstɪŋ/
horrible	/ˈhɔrəbəl/
hot	/hat/
large	/lardʒ/
noisy	/ˈnɔɪzi/
quiet	/ˈkwaɪət/
small	/ˈsmɔl/
wonderful	/ˈwʌndəfəl/

Modern History

Vocabulary • Ordinal numbers, years, dates

1 Listen. Match the numbers you hear to these words. Then listen and repeat.
3.1

fifth
first   *1*
fourth
second
third
thirty-first
twentieth
twenty-second

2 In pairs, ask and answer.

1 When is your birthday? *It's on May eighteenth.*
2 What is the date today?

3 Match the photos (1–8) to the events (a–h).

a The *Titanic* hits an iceberg. *1*
b Russia sends Laika the dog into space.
c Nelson Mandela leaves prison.
d Prince William marries Kate Middleton.
e Howard Carter discovers Tutankhamen's tomb
  in Egypt.
f The first space vehicle visits Mars.
g In Amsterdam, Anne Frank's family hide
  because of the war.
h People around the world celebrate
  the new millennium.

4 Match the events in Exercise 3 to these years.
3.2 **Then listen and check.**

nineteen forty-two	nineteen twelve *a*
nineteen twenty-two	two thousand eleven
two thousand	nineteen fifty-seven
nineteen ninety	two thousand four

Brain Trainer
Activity 3
Go to page 118

Reading

1 Look at the article and the photos. Are the photos from the 1960s, '70s or '80s?

2 Read the text. Match the photos (a–e) to the paragraphs (1–3).

3 Read and check your answers to Exercise 2.

4 3.3 Read the text again. Complete the events with the correct year.

Event 1	The Beatles' first song in the US	*1964*
Event 2	Twiggy on the cover of *Vogue*	
Event 3	TV in color for the first time	
Event 4	The first men on the moon	
Event 5	The Internet is invented	

5 3.3 Read the text again. Complete the sentences.

1 "I Want to Hold Your Hand" was a song by *The Beatles*.
2 In the 1960s people listened to music on the .... or on records.
3 The colors of .... in the 1960s were very bright.
4 The first fashion model in Madame Tussaud's was .... .
5 Some TV shows were in .... after 1967.
6 The first two men on the moon were .... .

6 What about you? **In pairs, ask and answer.**

1 What singers do your parents like?
2 Do you and your parents like the same music?
3 Do you have any photos of your parents or grandparents when they were young?

> What singers do your parents like?

> My dad likes Bob Dylan.

Flower Power!

1 What music was popular?
The Beatles were really popular in many countries. Their first song in the US was "I Want to Hold Your Hand" in January 1964. There weren't any MP3 players in the 1960s. There were radios and records!

2 What clothes were in fashion?
Clothes were very different! My grandparents were teenagers in the 1960s, so I have some great photos—look at these pants and shirts! Bright colors and flowers were very popular! Twiggy was the first international fashion model. She appeared on the cover of *Vogue* in the US in 1967, and she also modeled in France, Japan and the UK. She was the first model to appear in Madame Tussaud's wax museum in London.

3 What else?
Well, it was a time of change. Before 1967, TV was boring—it wasn't in color! The year 1969 was exciting! The Concorde's first flight was in April. Then on July 20, Neil Armstrong and Buzz Aldrin were the first men on the moon. In November, the system that became the Internet was invented in the US.

4 Is this an interesting time in history?
Yes, it is! It's fun to learn about different times and find out what people were like.

Grammar • Past simple: *to be*

Affirmative		
I	was	
He/She/It	was	in the café.
You/We/They	were	

Negative		
I	wasn't (was not)	
He/She/It	wasn't (was not)	at home.
You/We/They	weren't (were not)	

Questions		
Was	I	
Was	he/she/it	at school?
Were	you/we/they	

1 Study the grammar table. Copy and complete the table below.

To be		
	Present	**Past**
1	I am	I was
2	She is	*She was*
3	....	We were
4	They aren't	....
5	....	It wasn't
6	You aren't	....
7	Are you?	....
8	....	Was he?

2 Choose the correct options to complete the sentences.

At seven thirty last night …
1 Luke *was* / *were* at home.
2 Nick *wasn't* / *weren't* at his grandmother's house.
3 Lucia and Lidia *was* / *were* at the movies.
4 Luke's parents *wasn't* / *weren't* at a pizza place.
5 Lidia's dog *was* / *were* in the backyard.
6 Lucia's friends *wasn't* / *weren't* in the park.

• There was/There were

Affirmative	
There was a radio/some music.	
There were some children.	

Negative	
There wasn't a TV/any music.	
There weren't any computers.	

Questions and short answers	
Was there a phone/any music?	
Were there any phones?	
Yes, there was. / No, there wasn't.	
Yes, there were. / No, there weren't.	

Grammar reference Workbook page 98

3 Study the grammar table. Complete the rules.

1 We use .... and .... with singular nouns, e.g., *a radio*, to talk about the past.
2 We use .... and .... with plural nouns, e.g., *some computers*, to talk about the past.

4 Complete the questions and write the answers.
1 *Were* there any MP3 players 40 years ago? ✗
   No, there weren't.
2 *Was* there color TV 20 years ago? ✓
   Yes, there was.
3 .... there any cell phones 50 years ago? ✗
4 .... there a man on the moon in 1967? ✗
5 .... there any DVDs 10 years ago? ✓
6 .... there Internet 5 years ago? ✓
7 .... there email 30 years ago? ✗
8 .... there flowers on clothes in the 1960s? ✓

5 What about you? **Make sentences about things in your house five years ago. Use these words and/or your own ideas.**

There wasn't a guitar in my house five years ago.

DVDs	game console	guitar	laptop
parrot	rabbit	skateboard	

Vocabulary • Regular verbs

1 Match the pictures to these words. Then listen, check and repeat.

3.4

answer – answered	ask – asked	call – called
close – closed	invent – invented	like – liked
listen – listened	stop – stopped	study – studied
talk – talked	travel – traveled *1*	work – worked

Word list page 111 **Workbook** page 110

2 Match the phrases (1–4 and a–d) to make spelling rules for regular verbs.

1 Most verbs (e.g., *ask*) *b*
2 Final *-e* (e.g., *like*)
3 Final consonant + *-y* (e.g., *study*)
4 Short vowel + consonant (e.g., *stop*)

a Change *y* to *i*, then add *-ed*
b Add *-ed*
c Double consonant, add *-ed*
d Add *-d*

3 Match the other verbs in Exercise 1 to the spelling rules (1–4).

answer – 1

Pronunciation *-ed* endings

4a Listen to the *-ed* endings of these three regular verbs.

3.5 1 /d/ listened   2 /ɪd/ invented   3 /t/ talked

b Listen to these Past simple regular verbs. Which ending does each verb have: /d/, /ɪd/ or /t/?

3.6

1 started   2 watched   3 opened   4 asked   5 studied
6 wanted   7 worked   8 liked   9 called

c Listen again. Check your answers.

3.6

5 Complete the text with these words in the past. Then listen and check.

3.7

answer	ask	call
~~invent~~	like	listen
study	talk	travel
work		

Alexander Graham Bell
[1] *invented* the telephone in the 1870s. First, he [2] .... inventions from other inventors. Then he [3] .... with his friend, Mr. Watson. On June 2, 1872, Bell [4] .... Mr. Watson and [5] .... to him. Mr. Watson [6] ...., and Bell [7] ...., "Do you understand what I say?" "Yes," [8] .... Mr. Watson. Bell's words [9] .... sixteen kilometers. It was the first "long-distance" phone call. People [10] .... Bell's idea. The phone changed their lives.

6 Complete the sentences with verbs from Exercise 1.

1 Can I *ask* you a question?
2 Please, can you .... the door?
3 I can't .... the question.
4 Do you .... your new camera?

7 Write three sentences about yesterday. Use the verbs from Exercise 1.

I called Irina yesterday.

**Brain Trainer
Activity 4**
Go to page 118

Speaking and Listening

1 Look at the photo. What things does Julia's grandma have?

2 Listen and read the conversation. Are the statements true (T) or false (F)?
3.8

1 Julia's grandma is reading a book. *F*
2 Julia's grandma lived with her sister for a year while her husband was in Vietnam.
3 Julia's grandpa mailed a lot of letters.
4 Julia's grandpa often called Julia's grandma.
5 It was cheap to make a phone call.
6 The phone booth wasn't near the house.
7 Julia's grandparents moved to where they live now two years ago.
8 Julia's grandparents watched TV every evening.
9 They liked pop music.

3 Act out the conversation in groups of three.

Julia	Hello, Grandma! Sorry I didn't visit you last weekend. What are you doing?
Grandma	I'm reading some old letters from your grandpa. You know, I lived with my sister for two years while he was in Vietnam. He mailed a letter to me every week … but he didn't call me very often.
Julia	Why not?
Grandpa	Because it was expensive!
Grandma	And the phone was in a phone booth three kilometers away!
Julia	What a pain!
Grandma	Then I moved here in the 1970s. That was about forty years ago.
Grandpa	I remember. In those days, we listened to the radio every evening.
Julia	Really? What was your favorite music?
Grandma	We loved rock'n'roll.

Say it in your language …
What a pain!

4 **Look back at the conversation. Who says what?**

1 I didn't visit you last weekend. *Julia*
2 I lived with my sister for two years.
3 I moved here in the 1970s.
4 That was forty years ago.
5 In those days, we listened to the radio.

 5 **Read the phrases for talking about the past.**

Past-time expressions
last weekend
for two years
in the 1970s
forty years ago
in those days

 6 **Listen to the conversations. Act out the conversations in pairs.**
3.9

Steven Where were you ¹last weekend? Were you at home?
Nina No, I wasn't. I was ²at my grandparents' house.

Jason I wasn't at school ¹yesterday morning.
Sonia Really? Why not?
Jason Because I was ²sick.

7 **Work in pairs. Replace the words in purple in Exercise 6 with these words. Act out the conversations.**

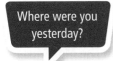
Where were you yesterday?

I was at a friend's house.

1 last night / last week / last Friday

2 at the movies / in Hawaii / at school

1 yesterday afternoon / last Thursday / three days ago

2 at the doctor's office / at the dentist's office / at home in bed

8 **Act out the conversation again with your own words and ideas.**

Grammar • Past simple regular: affirmative and negative

Affirmative	
I/You/He/She/It/We/They	listened.
	danced.
	studied.
	traveled.

Negative	
I/You/He/She/It/We/They	didn't (did not) listen.
	didn't (did not) dance.
	didn't (did not) study.
	didn't (did not) travel.

Grammar reference Workbook page 98

 1 **Study the grammar table. Answer the questions to complete the rules.**

1 Is the third person (He/She/It) different in the Past simple?
2 How do we make the Past simple negative?

 2 **Complete the sentences with the Past simple affirmative.**

1 Yesterday she .... (clean up) her room.
2 We .... (carry) the computer to the classroom.
3 The actors .... (dance) in that movie.
4 Our dog .... (jump) in the car this morning.
5 My friends and I .... (walk) to school last week.
6 We .... (watch) a DVD last night.
7 The bus .... (stop) near the museum.

 3 **Put the sentences in Exercise 2 in the negative form.**

1 *Yesterday she didn't clean up her room.*

 4 **Complete the text with these verbs in the Past simple.**

clean up	get	not help	not like
not watch	play	~~stay~~	want

Last night my parents were out, so I ¹ *stayed* at home with my brother, Harry. I ² .... the living room, but Harry ³ .... me. Next, I ⁴ .... games with him, but he ⁵ .... the games. Then he ⁶ .... to watch *Jaws*, a scary movie about a shark. We ⁷ .... it for long. When Mom and Dad ⁸ .... home, my brother and I were behind the sofa!

Reading

1 Look at the names (1–6). Can you match them to the photos (a–f)?

1 *Jaws*
2 *Grease*
3 ABBA
4 *ET*
5 Andy Warhol
6 Michael Jackson

Travel Back in Time!

Welcome to the Time Tunnels at **The Max Museum of Modern Culture!**

In the first Time Tunnel, you can relive the culture of the '70s. This was a time of freedom for women and young people in America and Western Europe. Andy Warhol was a famous pop artist. His career started in the '60s, but he was popular in the '70s because his work was fresh and modern.

At that time, people watched exciting movies like *Jaws*, *Star Wars* and *Grease*. In the evening, people enjoyed disco music. They danced to ABBA, the European superstars from Sweden. Some movie posters and record covers from the '70s are pieces of art now.

In the second Time Tunnel, you can visit the '80s. American culture was "cool" in that decade; many people liked fast food and Hollywood blockbuster movies like *ET* and *Wall Street*. People worked long hours, and some young people wanted a lot of money, but others didn't like this culture of "Me, me, me." Graffiti art was one way to show that they were angry.

In the '80s, people enjoyed some great pop music—for example, Madonna and Michael Jackson. Their videos and stage shows were also a type of art.

Key Words		
tunnel	culture	freedom
fresh	blockbuster	angry

2 Read and check your answers to Exercise 1.

3 Read the text quickly. Are these people and things
3.10 from the '70s or '80s Time Tunnel?

a Graffiti art *'80s Time Tunnel*
b Andy Warhol
c *Wall Street*
d Madonna
e *Star Wars*
f ABBA

4 Read the text again. Answer the questions.
3.10 1 What type of museum is it?
   It is a museum of modern culture.
2 Who was Andy Warhol?
3 Which Swedish band was famous for disco music?
4 What were two examples of American culture?
5 Why was graffiti art popular in the '80s?

Listening

1 Listen to three people from The Max Museum.
3.11 Match each speaker to the thing he/she does.

Speaker 1
Speaker 2
Speaker 3
a take photographs
b sell tickets
c work in the gift shop

2 Listen again and find these things.
3.11 1 names of two famous people
2 three colors
3 a number

3 What about you? **Imagine you are in the year 2030. In pairs, say what the year 2014 was like.**

Writing • An essay

1 Read the Writing File.

> **Writing File** Punctuation 2
>
> - We use **periods (.)** at the end of a sentence.
> - We use **commas (,)** to make a pause in the middle of a sentence, e.g., before *but*.
> - We use **question marks (?)** at the end of a question. Be careful! We don't use question marks at the beginning of a question.
> - We use **exclamation points (!)** to express surprise.

2 Read Jason's essay. What punctuation (1–5) is missing?

When I Was Young

The "noughties" (2000–2009) were a good time to be young ¹ [.] There were some great TV shows for kids, like the Japanese cartoon *Yu-Gi-Oh*. *Yu-Gi-Oh* was about Yugi, a high school student with a Pharaoh's spirit. I loved it!
There were also some good movies a few years ago. The Harry Potter movies were very popular, and I was a big fan. I didn't see them at the theater, but I watched them on DVD a lot of times ² [...] My favorite character was Ron Weasley ³ [...] but I didn't like Lord Voldemort.
Was there any good music in the noughties ⁴ [...] I think so. I liked Linkin Park ⁵ [...] but music in the twenty-tens is better. My Chemical Romance and The Wanted are amazing!

Jason, Australia

3 Read the essay again. Answer the questions.

1 When were the "noughties"?
   The "noughties" were from 2000 to 2009.
2 Which country was the show *Yu-Gi-Oh* from?
3 Was Jason a Harry Potter fan?
4 Who was his favorite character?
5 Which was his favorite band in the "noughties"?
6 What bands does Jason like now?

4 Rewrite the sentences with commas (if necessary) and a period or a question mark.

1 The song was old but it was very popular
   The song was old, but it was very popular.
2 Who was in the Harry Potter movies
3 How old were you in 2010
4 We watched TV yesterday afternoon
5 I liked *Pokémon* but I didn't like *Yu-Gi-Oh*

5 Think about when you were young. Take notes about these things. Give reasons.

1 TV shows you liked – and why
2 movies you liked – and why
3 singers and bands you liked – and why

6 Write an essay titled "When I Was Young."
Use "My essay" and your notes from Exercise 5.

> **My essay**
>
> **Paragraph 1**
> 1 Say what time you are writing about.
> 2 Say what shows you liked.
>
> **Paragraph 2**
> 3 Say what movies you liked.
>
> **Paragraph 3**
> 4 Say what music you liked.
> 5 Compare it with music you like now.

> **Remember!**
> - Use punctuation correctly.
> - Use the vocabulary in this unit.
> - Check your grammar, spelling and punctuation.

Refresh Your Memory!

Grammar • Review

1 Complete the text with *was/wasn't* or *were/weren't*.

• Which countries ¹ *were* in the "Space Race"?

In the 1950s and '60s, Russia and America ² ....
in a "Space Race." The first man in space ³ ....
Yuri Gagarin from Russia.

• Which country ⁴ .... first on the moon?

The first rocket on the moon ⁵ .... American. It was
the Russian Luna 2 in 1959, but there weren't any
people in this rocket. The first men on the moon
⁶ .... from Russia. They were from America.
The date ⁷ .... July 20, 1969. Buzz Aldrin and Neil
Armstrong ⁸ .... on the moon for 21 hours.

2 Make sentences with *There was/were* or *There wasn't/weren't*.

1 an MP3 player on the table
   There was an MP3 player on the table.
2 not any songs on the MP3 player
3 some DVDs next to a laptop
4 not a car in the garage
5 a cell phone on the chair
6 some text messages on the phone

3 Make sentences with the Past simple.

1 Jake / visit / his friend in the hospital yesterday
   Jake visited his friend in the hospital yesterday.
2 Angelina / play / soccer with her brother
3 We / call / our grandparents last night
4 Sam and Sara / study / for their math test
5 The students / answer / the teacher's questions
6 The car / stop / near the park

4 Correct the sentences.

1 Howard Carter discovered Tutankhamen's
   tomb in Greece. (Egypt)
   *He didn't discover Tutankhamen's tomb
   in Greece. He discovered it in Egypt.*
2 The first space vehicle visited Mars in 2012. (2004)
3 People celebrated the millennium in 1998. (2000)
4 Alexander Graham Bell invented the MP3
   player. (telephone)
5 Anne Frank's family lived in Paris. (Amsterdam)

Vocabulary • Review

5 Write the dates in full in your notebook.

1 4/20/1982
   April twentieth, nineteen eighty-two
2 3/10/2030
3 8/3/1861
4 1/21/2018
5 10/2/2003
6 8/1/1999

6 Match the verbs (1–4) to the correct Past simple spelling rules (a–d).

1 dance / love
2 chop / plan
3 play / clean
4 study / hurry

a add *-ed*
b change *-y* to *-i*, add *-ed*
c double the consonant, add *-ed*
d add *-d*

Speaking • Review

7 Complete the conversations with a past time word. Then listen and check.
3.12

last	ago	yesterday

Adam Where's Mom?
Erin I don't know. She was here
         half an hour ¹ .... .

Ivan Where were you ² .... night?
        Were you at the gym?
Eva No, I wasn't. I was at home.

Dina Why didn't you go to school ³ .... ?
Paulo Because I was at the doctor's office.

Dictation

8 Listen and write in your notebook.
3.13

My assessment profile: Workbook page 133

Twenty-Four Hours in the Life of a Roman Child

The day started with breakfast. For rich Romans, there was bread, fish, meat, fruit and honey. Slaves prepared and served the food. For poor Romans, breakfast was different. They had bread with water.

Then it was time to go to school. School started really early—before sunrise—and it got out late! Schools weren't big. There was usually one tutor and a small group of children. At school, children studied reading, writing and math. They used small stones to do math problems. They practiced writing on wax tablets—they scratched the words onto the wax with a pointed stick.

Most children finished school when they were 10 or 11, but some children continued to a "Grammar school." Here they studied Latin, Greek, grammar and literature. They also practiced public speaking. Some children studied at home. Their teachers were the family's slaves. The slaves were often smart and well-educated, and they were good teachers.

After school, children played with toys at home. The boys often played war games and practiced fighting. Some Roman toys are very similar to modern toys. Roman children played with dolls, hoops, kites and stilts.

Reading

1 **Read the text quickly. What do you think it is about?**

a Roman food
b Roman daily life
c Education in Rome today

2 **Read the text again. Answer the questions.**
3.14
1 What did rich people have for breakfast?
People had bread, fish, meat, fruit and honey.
2 Who prepared the food for rich people?
3 Were schools big or small?
4 What did children study at school?
5 Who taught children at home?
6 What did children play with at home?

My History File

3 **Do some research into the daily life of a child from ancient Egypt. Find the answers to these questions:**

- When did he/she get up?
- When did he/she go to bed?
- What did he/she eat?
- What did he/she do?

4 **Write a short paragraph about the daily life of an ancient Egyptian child in your notebook. Use your notes from Exercise 3 to help you.**

Travel

Grammar
Past simple irregular:
affirmative and negative;
Past simple: questions

Vocabulary
Means of transportation;
Clothes

Speaking
Talking on the phone

Writing
A travel diary

Word list page 111
Workbook page 111

Vocabulary • Means of transportation

1 Match the vehicles in the picture to these words. Then listen, check and repeat.
3.15

> bike
> boat
> bus
> canoe
> car *1*
> helicopter
> motorcycle
> plane
> scooter
> subway
> train
> truck
> van

2 Which means of transportation from Exercise 1
3.16 can you hear? Listen and say.

   1 *It's a boat.*

3 Where do you usually use each means
of transportation? Complete the list.

   1 on land: **2 on water:**   **3 in the air:**
   car, … .   *boat, … .*   *plane, … .*

4 Match the verbs to the nouns.

   1 take   a a plane
   2 sail   b a train
   3 drive   c a bike, a motorcycle
   4 fly   d a boat
   5 ride   e a car

5 In pairs, make up an unusual route from your
home to another country. You must use at least
five different means of transportation.

> First, we ride our bikes
> to the bus stop. Next, we take a
> bus to the river. Then we …

**Brain Trainer
Activity 4**
Go to page 119

Reading

1 Look at the extracts (a–c) from *Around the World in Eighty Days* by Jules Verne. Guess: what is it about?

a Phileas Fogg can't find his bag. Is it in France? Is it in China? He travels to 80 countries. But where is his bag?

b It is 1872. Phileas Fogg's friends say, "No one can travel around the world in 80 days." "I can!" says Phileas Fogg. And his adventure begins.

c Phileas Fogg works at a train station. He meets many people from different countries. He hears 80 stories from 80 places around the world, but he never travels.

2 Read and check your ideas to Exercise 1.

3 Read the text quickly. Put the events in the correct order.
3.17

a Passepartout gets a bag for Phileas Fogg.
b Phileas Fogg goes into his house.
c Phileas Fogg leaves the Club. *1*
d Phileas Fogg and Passepartout get on a train.
e Phileas Fogg says goodbye to his friends.
f Phileas Fogg sees his friends at the station.
g Phileas Fogg gives his bag to Passepartout.

4 Read the text again. Answer the questions.
3.17
1 Where are Phileas Fogg's friends at the beginning of the extract? *They are at the Club.*
2 Where does Phileas Fogg live?
3 Phileas Fogg asks Passepartout for two things. What are they?
4 What does Phileas Fogg put inside the bag?
5 Where are Phileas Fogg's friends at the end of the extract?
6 What time do Phileas Fogg and Passepartout leave Charing Cross Station?

5 What about you? **In pairs, ask and answer.**

1 Do you like traveling?
2 Imagine you are traveling around the world in 80 days. What do you want to put in your suitcase?

Around the World in Eighty Days

At 7:25, Phileas Fogg said good night to his friends and left the Club. At 7:50, he opened the door of his house in Savile Row and went in.

"Mr. Fogg? Is that you?" said Passepartout.

"We must go to Charing Cross Station immediately. I want to make a trip around the world."

Passepartout didn't understand him.

"Around the world?" he asked.

"In eighty days," said Phileas Fogg. "We must go now. Now!"

"But your bags?"

"I need one small bag. Bring my coat. Wear strong shoes. Move!"

At eight o'clock, Passepartout was ready with a small bag. "A quiet life," he thought. "Where is my quiet life?"

Phileas Fogg didn't have a lot of things for the trip. He took the bag from Passepartout and put a lot of money, and a train and ship schedule, into it. Then he gave the bag to Passepartout.

At the station, Phileas Fogg saw his five friends from the Club.

"You're here to say goodbye? That's kind," he said.

At 8:40, Phileas Fogg and Passepartout got on the train, and at 8:45 the train started.

Grammar • Past simple irregular: affirmative and negative

Base	Affirmative	Negative
buy	bought	didn't (did not) buy
do	did	didn't (did not) do
get	got	didn't (did not) get
give	gave	didn't (did not) give
go	went	didn't (did not) go
have	had	didn't (did not) have
put	put	didn't (did not) put
take	took	didn't (did not) take
think	thought	didn't (did not) think
understand	understood	didn't (did not) understand

Watch Out!
They went to Paris last month.
You didn't go to Orlando last month.
BUT:
I was in New Jersey yesterday.
We were in Rome yesterday.

He wasn't in Rome yesterday.
They weren't in New Jersey yesterday.

Go to page 127 **for a full list of irregular Past simple verbs**

Grammar reference Workbook page 100

1 Study the grammar table. Complete the rule.

For the Past simple negative form, we put the word .... before the base verb.

2 Are these Past simple verbs regular (R) or irregular (I)?

buy – bought /	drink – drank	give – gave
live – lived	say – said	see – saw
study – studied	visit – visited	work – worked

3 Complete the text below with the Past simple.

I ¹ *went* (go) downtown with my friend Elizabeth last weekend. We ² .... (see) a great movie at the theater. After the movie, we ³ .... (go) shopping. I ⁴ .... (buy) a new game for my game console. My friend ⁵ .... (get) a book about computers. Then we ⁶ .... (eat) some pizza at a pizza place. At seven o'clock, we ⁷ .... (take) the bus home. We ⁸ .... (have) a great day.

4 Rewrite the verbs from Exercise 3 in the Past simple negative.

1 *I didn't go.*

5 Complete the article.

True Stories: I Changed My Life

Jane Fletcher before   Jane Fletcher now

Jane Fletcher is healthier and happier today. Why? She changed her life.

Now she ¹ *walks* (walk) to work every day, but two years ago she ² *didn't walk* (not walk) to work; she ³ *went* (go) by car. Now she ⁴ .... (have) cereal for breakfast, but two years ago she ⁵ .... (not have) cereal for breakfast; she ⁶ .... (have) cake. Now she ⁷ .... (go to bed) at ten o'clock, but two years ago she ⁸ .... (not go to bed) at ten o'clock; she ⁹ .... (go to bed) at midnight. Now she ¹⁰ .... (ride) her bike in the park on the weekend, but two years ago, she ¹¹ .... (not ride) her bike; she drove her car downtown on the weekend.

6 **What about you?** Write three true statements about something you changed in your life.

Vocabulary • Clothes

1 Match the pictures to these words. Then listen,
3.18 check and repeat.

boots	coat	dress *1*	hat
jeans	pajamas	pants	sandals
scarf	shoes	shorts	skirt
sneakers	sweater	T-shirt	

Word list page 111
Workbook page 111

2 Copy and put the clothes words in Exercise 1 into
3.19 the correct category. Then listen, check and repeat.

a top half of body
  coat, ... , ...
b bottom half of body
  .... , ... , ... , ...
c whole body
  .... , ...
d feet
  .... , ... , ... , ...
e head and neck
  .... , ...

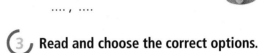

3 Read and choose the correct options.

In winter I usually wear ¹ *jeans* / *shorts*,
a ² *T-shirt* / *sweater* and ³ *sandals* / *boots*.
When I go outside, I always wear a ⁴ *skirt* / *coat*,
and sometimes I have a ⁵ *hat* / *scarf* around my
neck, too. Today it's very hot and sunny, so I'm
wearing a summer ⁶ *sweater* / *dress*. My sister
isn't feeling well, so she's still in bed, and she's
wearing her ⁷ *sneakers* / *pajamas*.

4 Listen. Who is Ben's sister?
3.20

a Dolly   b Molly   c Holly

5 Choose one person in the class. Describe his/her
clothes to your partner. Can your partner guess
who the person is?

**Brain Trainer
Activity 5**
Go to page 119

Chatroom Talking on the phone

Speaking and Listening

1 **Look at the photos. Answer the questions.**

1 Is Julia happy or sad?
2 What is Nick doing?

2 **Listen and read the conversation.**
3.21 **Answer the questions.**

1 Who is Mr. Davies? *Nick's dad*
2 Who does Julia want to speak to?
3 Where is Julia?
4 What does Julia want to do on Saturday?
5 Where did Julia wear her scarf yesterday?
6 What does Julia want to do this evening?

3 **Act out the conversation in groups of three.**

Mr. Davies	Hello?
Julia	Hi, is this Nick?
Mr. Davies	No, it isn't. This is his dad. Who's this?
Julia	Hi, Mr. Davies, it's Julia. Can I speak to Nick, please?
Mr. Davies	Hello, Julia! Hold on ... Nick! Just a minute ... here he is.
Nick	Hi, Julia! Where are you?
Julia	I'm at home. Listen, I can't find my favorite purple scarf, and I want to wear it on Saturday. Did I leave it at your house?
Nick	I don't know. Did you wear it to school yesterday?
Julia	Yes, I did. But it's not there. I checked this morning. Can I come to your house this evening? I want to look for it.
Nick	Sure. See you later. Bye!
Julia	Bye!

Say it in your language ...
Just a minute.
Listen, ...

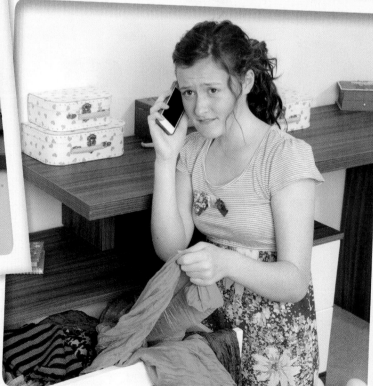

4 Look back at the conversation. How does Julia ask to speak to Nick? How does Mr. Davies ask Julia to wait?

5 Read the phrases for talking on the phone.

Talking on the phone
Hi / Hello, is this … ?
Who's this?
It's … .
Can I speak to … , please?
Hold on.
Just a minute.
Here he is.
See you later.
Bye!

Pronunciation Sounding polite

6a Listen. Who is more polite, Emma or Valerie?

3.22

Henry	Hello.
Emma	Hello, is this Frank?
Henry	No, it's Henry.
Emma	Hi, Henry, it's Emma. Can I speak to Frank, please?
Henry	Hello.
Valerie	Hello, Henry, it's Valerie.
Henry	Hi, Valerie.
Valerie	Can I speak to Frank, please?

b Listen again and repeat.
3.22

7 Listen to the conversations. Act out
3.23 the conversations in pairs.

Nick	Hello.
Leo	Hi, Nick, it's Leo. Can I speak to Ted, please?
Nick	Hold on.
Mrs. Green	Hello.
Monica	Hello, is this Rebecca?
Mrs. Green	No, it isn't. This is her mother.
Monica	Oh, sorry. Can I speak to Rebecca, please?
Mrs. Green	Of course. Here she is.

Grammar • Past simple: questions

Questions and short answers
Did I/you/he/she/it/we/they read the book?
Yes, I/you/he/she/it/we/they did.
No, I/you/he/she/it/we/they didn't.

Wh questions
Where did I/you/he/she/it/we/they go yesterday?
I went to the movies.

Grammar reference Workbook page 100

1 Study the grammar table. Complete the rule.

We make Past simple questions with …. + *I / you / he / she / it / we / they* + verb.

2 Read Jamie's answers and complete
3.24 the questions. Then listen and check.

1 Where *did you go* (go) last weekend?
   I went to Seattle.
2 How …. there? (get)
   I flew there.
3 What …. in Seattle? (do)
   I climbed the Space Needle.
4 When …. ? (leave)
   I left on Sunday evening.
5 …. home? (fly)
   No, I didn't. I came home by bus.

3 Make questions and answers.

A you / meet / Jane / yesterday?
B I / have / lunch with her. Then / we / go / to the movies
A Did you meet Jane yesterday?
B Yes, I did. I had lunch with her. Then …
A What / movie / you / see?
B We / see / the new Kristen Stewart movie
A you / enjoy it?
B I / not like / it. I / think / it / be / really boring

4 In pairs, find out about your partner's favorite vacation. Use these ideas.

do some painting	go kayaking
go rollerblading	go to museums
listen to music	meet with friends
play tennis	stay in a hotel

Reading

1 **Look at the photo. Where do you think these people live?**

a in a village b in a tent c in a big city

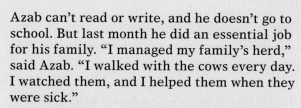

AZAB'S JOURNEY

Azab is thirteen years old. He lives in Niger, in West Africa, but he doesn't live in a village or a town, and his family doesn't have a house. Azab is a Wodaabe nomad. There are more than 40,000 Wodaabe people in Niger. They live in simple tents, and they travel every two or three days. They follow the rain and move to places with water and grass for their cattle. The cows are very important for the Wodaabe people because cows' milk is their main food. They make yogurt and butter with the milk, and when they are near a village, they sell the milk and buy other food.

Azab can't read or write, and he doesn't go to school. But last month he did an essential job for his family. "I managed my family's herd," said Azab. "I walked with the cows every day. I watched them, and I helped them when they were sick."

Last year Azab's family traveled more than 3,000 kilometers around West Africa. "There was no rain," said Azab. "We went from one place to another place. We didn't find food and we were hungry. It was a very difficult time."

Key Words		
nomad	to follow	cattle
essential	to manage	herd

2 **Read and check your answer to Exercise 1.**

 3 **Read the text quickly. Choose the correct description.**

3.25

Wodaabe nomads …
a live in villages in Niger and sell cows.
b travel around West Africa and don't have houses.
c move to different places because they don't have cows.

 4 **Read the text again. Answer the questions.**

3.25

1 How old is Azab? *Azab is thirteen years old.*
2 How many Wodaabe people live in Niger?
3 Why do they move to different places?
4 What do they usually eat?
5 What did Azab do last month?
6 Why was life difficult for Azab's family last year?

Listening

 1 **Listen to Rose's conversation with Erik. Answer the questions.**

3.26

1 Did Rose have a good day or a bad day?
2 Where is she now?

 2 **Listen again. Are the statements true (T) or false (F)?**

3.26

1 Rose got up late because she didn't hear her alarm clock. *T*
2 Rose took the bus to school.
3 Rose liked her trip to school today.
4 Rose got to school late.
5 Rose's teacher was angry because she didn't have her homework.
6 Rose is doing her homework now.

Writing • A travel diary

1 **Read the Writing File.**

> **Writing File** Paragraphs
>
> - We use paragraphs to organize our writing. We start a new paragraph when we introduce a new topic.
> - A new paragraph starts on a new line, usually after a space.

2 **Read the travel diary. Match the paragraphs (A–C) to the descriptions (1–3).**

1 Summary of the day
2 Description of the Taj Mahal
3 Description of the journey to Agra

My Indian Diary by Jamie Weller

Monday

A Today we traveled 200 kilometers from New Delhi to the Taj Mahal in Agra. We went by bus, and the trip took three hours. It was very hot, and there were a lot of people, but we enjoyed it.

B When we arrived at the Taj Mahal, we were amazed. It looks beautiful in photographs, but it's even more beautiful in real life! Our guide talked about the history of the building, and then we walked around it.

C We returned to New Delhi in the evening. We were very tired when we got back to our hotel, but it was a fantastic day. The Taj Mahal is awesome!

3 **Read the diary again. Answer the questions.**

1 How far is Agra from New Delhi?
   It is 200 kilometers.
2 Did Jamie like traveling on the bus?
3 What did they do when they arrived at the Taj Mahal?
4 Did they stay in Agra on Monday night?

4 **Read the text and divide it into paragraphs.**

Paragraph 1 Description of the market
Paragraph 2 Description of the Lodi Gardens
Paragraph 3 Summary of the day

Tuesday

We got up early today and walked to the Dilli Haat market. The market is interesting. You can buy a lot of different things there. I loved the clothes, and my sister liked the food! We took a bus from the market to Lodi Gardens. They are really beautiful. We had a picnic and watched the birds. I loved the shopping in the morning, and the gardens were amazing.

5 **Imagine you are on a trip. Answer the questions.**

1 What did you see?
2 What did you buy?
3 Did you enjoy the experience? Why?/Why not?

Places to visit
museums / interesting buildings / the beach / an amusement park / a palace / a park / gardens

Adjectives
Positive: interesting / amazing / great
Negative: noisy / horrible / dirty

Things to do
buy souvenirs / swim in the ocean / visit museums

6 **Write your travel diary. Use "My diary" and your notes from Exercise 5.**

> **My diary**
>
> **Paragraph 1**
> *Yesterday / Last summer I went to … .*
> *We went by bus / train / plane.*
> *We saw … .*
> **Paragraph 2**
> *I / My sister / My mother bought … .*
> **Paragraph 3**
> *It was interesting / great / horrible … .*

> **Remember!**
> - Divide your writing into paragraphs.
> - Use the vocabulary in this unit.
> - Check your grammar, spelling and punctuation.

Refresh Your Memory!

Grammar • Review

1 Choose the correct options.

1 I *didn't understand / not understood* the homework, so I *didn't do / not did* it.
2 Mary *speak / spoke* to Jason yesterday.
3 We *saw / see* your cousin on his motorcycle this morning.
4 He *go / went* to Miami by plane.
5 My friends *didn't / don't* take the bus to school yesterday; they *take / took* the subway.

2 Complete the text with the Past simple form of the verbs.

Last Saturday I ¹ *had* (have) a picnic with my uncle and my cousins. We ² .... (drink) fruit smoothies, and we ³ .... (have) some delicious sandwiches. After the food, we all ⁴ .... (sing) songs together. It ⁵ .... (be) a wonderful day.

3 Put the words in the correct order to make questions.

1 my message / Did / you / to Tom / give / ?
   Did you give my message to Tom?
2 you / at the supermarket / did / What / buy / ?
3 your friends / at midnight / leave / the party / Did / ?
4 books / How many / read / last year / you / did / ?
5 Sarah / on the math test / get / 100% / Did / ?
6 Where / go / did / on vacation / you / ?

4 Make questions and answers.

1 you / go to the park / yesterday?
   No. I / go to the gym
   Did you go to the park yesterday?
   No, I didn't. I went to the gym.
2 you / play tennis with Peter / at the gym?
   No. we / go swimming
3 you and Peter / have lunch / at the café?
   No. we / have lunch / at Peter's house
4 you / take the bus home / after lunch?
   No. I / walk / home
5 you / do your homework / in the afternoon?
   No. I / listen / to music
6 you / send an email to Eva / in the evening?
   No. I / call Eva

Vocabulary • Review

5 Complete the transportation sentences with the missing letters.

1 *Cars*, t _ _ _ _ _ and v _ _ _ d _ _ _ _ on land.
2 B _ _ _ _ s _ _ _ on water.
3 P _ _ _ _ _ and h _ _ _ _ _ _ _ _ _ _ f _ _ in the air.

6 Read and match.

1 You wear these on your feet when you play sports.   a dress
2 You wear these on your feet in the summer.   b sandals
3 You wear this on the top half of your body.   c scarf
4 You wear them in bed.   d sneakers
5 Girls wear this.   e sweater
6 You wear this on your head.   f pants
7 You wear this around your neck.   g hat
8 You wear them on your legs.   h pajamas

Speaking • Review

7 Complete the phone conversation with these words. Then listen and check.
3.27

Bye	Can I speak	Hold on
~~is this~~	See you later	Who's speaking

Tina Hello.
James Hello, ¹ *is this* Maddy?
Tina No, it's Tina. ² .... , please?
James Hi, Tina, it's James. ³ .... to Maddy, please?
Tina Sure. ⁴ .... . Here she is.
Maddy Hi, James.
James Hi, Maddy. I'm bored. Can I come over to your house this afternoon?
Maddy Yes, of course.
James OK, then. ⁵ .... . Bye.
Maddy ⁶ .... .

Dictation

8 Listen and write in your notebook.
3.28

 My assessment profile: Workbook page 134

Phiona Mutesi's Profile

Age	Home country
17	Uganda

City

Kampala

Phiona's Journey

Phiona Mutesi is from a poor part of Uganda, and she left school when she was 8 years old. The following year, when she was 9, she joined a chess club at her church. Her brothers went there, and she followed them. At first she didn't know what chess was, but she liked the chess pieces! She practiced every evening at home with her brothers, and she soon became very good at the game.

In 2007 Phiona entered her first tournament. She was 11 years old, and she played chess against people ages 18, 19 and 20. Some people laughed at her because her clothes were simple, and she was poor. But she won the tournament, and people stopped laughing.

In 2009, when she was 13 years old, Phiona Mutesi made her first trip to another country. She traveled on a plane from her home in Uganda to Juba in South Sudan to play chess in an international tournament with children from 16 other countries. She won all her games, and she won the girls' title.

Now she is the No. 2 chess player in Uganda. Her teacher, Robert Katende, says, "In chess, it does not matter where you come from. Only where you put the pieces."

Reading

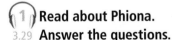

1 **Read about Phiona.**

3.29 **Answer the questions.**

1 When did Phiona leave school?
When she was 8 years old.

2 Where did she learn to play chess?

3 How did she become good at the game?

4 Why did some people laugh at Phiona?

5 Did Phiona win the chess tournament in 2007?

6 When did she go to Juba?

7 How many countries did the children at the tournament come from?

Class discussion

● Is there a chess club in your city, town or school?

● What do you like to do after school?

● Imagine Phiona's trip to Juba. What things were new or unusual for her?

Technology Time

Vocabulary • Technology

1 Match the objects in the photos to these words. Then listen, check and repeat.

3.30

blog
broadband
digital radio
e-reader *1*
flash drive
IM (instant messaging)
interactive whiteboard
netbook
screen
smart phone
social networking site
Wi-Fi

2 Complete the sentences with words from Exercise 1.

1 I did my homework on my home computer, then I took it to school on a f*lash drive*.
2 I don't use a laptop. I use a n .... because it's smaller.
3 You can talk to a lot of friends and share photos on a s .... .
4 It's faster to go on the Internet with b .... .
5 The s .... on a cell phone is very small.
6 You can use a W .... Internet connection in many different places.
7 My dad always listens to the sports news on his d .... .

3 Read the definition and say the word.

1 Teachers sometimes write on this in the classroom. *interactive whiteboard*
2 This is a fast way to send short messages.
3 This is a cell phone which has email and an MP3 player.
4 This isn't a paper book. It's electronic.
5 This is an online diary.

4 In pairs, ask and answer about technology.

Do you use IM?

Yes, I sometimes/often use it.

Brain Trainer Activity 3
Go to page 120

No, I never use it.

Reading

1 Look at the text and the photos. What do you think the text is about?

  a The future of novels
  b E-readers vs cell phones
  c The future of reading

2 Read the text and check your answer to Exercise 1.

3 3.31 Read the text again. Add the words or sentences (a–c) to the paragraphs (1–3).

  a Why don't you write one today?
  b They're going to be waterproof too, so we can read in the bathtub!
  c phone texts, instant messages and short messages on social networking sites.

4 3.31 Read the text again. Complete the sentences with one word from the text.

  1 These days people often read text on a *screen*.
  2 Soon, e-readers are going to …. .
  3 E-readers with flexible screens are …. .
  4 In the future, e-books can have 3-D …. .
  5 "Keitai" are popular in …. .
  6 You read "keitai" novels on a …. .
  7 Twitter novels are very …. .

5 What about you? In pairs, ask and answer.

  1 Do you read paper books or e-books?
  2 Which is better, an e-book or a paper book?
  3 Can you write a Twitter novel?

> Do you read paper books, e-books or no books?

> I read paper books. I love reading!

E-Reading!

e-reading!

1 We use computers all the time, and we read text on a screen every day—[1] …. Many people use their cell phone to read, and some have e-readers. What do you use? What are you going to use in the future?

2 E-readers are going to change in the future. We know that producers of e-readers are going to give them flexible screens so they're soft and easy to carry. [2] …. But what are we going to see after that? Imagine a new generation of e-readers that can read you a story, e-books that can change color, e-books with 3-D pictures. All of them are going to be possible.

3 What about books for cell phones? In Japan, "keitai" are popular. These are very short novels for people to read on their cell phones. Even teenagers can become writers of "keitai" novels. Many people also like the new fashion for Twitter novels. These are only 140 characters long—that's shorter than this paragraph! [3] ….

Grammar • Be going to

Affirmative		
I	'm (am)	going to read an e-book on the weekend.
You/We/They	're (are)	
He/She/It	's (is)	

Negative		
I	'm not (am not)	going to use IM this evening.
You/We/They	aren't (are not)	
He/She/It	isn't (is not)	

Questions and short answers		
Am	I	going to buy a laptop tomorrow?
Are	you/we/they	
Is	he/she/it	

Yes, I am. / No, I'm not.
Yes, you/we/they are. / No, you/we/they aren't.
Yes, he/she/it is. / No, he/she/it isn't.

Watch Out!
Use *be going to* with these expressions:
tomorrow, next week, next month, next year, soon

Grammar reference Workbook page 102

1 Study the grammar table. Complete the rules.

1 Before *going to,* we use the verb .... .
2 To make the negative, we add .... before *going to.*
3 In the question form, the first words are .... .

2 Complete the sentences with the affirmative of *be going to.*

1 I *'m going to stay* (stay) with my grandparents this summer.
2 Ella .... (climb) Sydney Harbor Bridge next month.
3 Nina's family .... (fly) to Rio de Janeiro on the weekend.
4 Omar and his mom .... (visit) the Leaning Tower of Pisa tomorrow.
5 My dad .... (run) a marathon next week.

3 The sentences in Exercise 2 are false. Rewrite them in the negative.

1 *I'm not going to stay with my grandparents this summer.*

4 You are going to interview people at a technology fair. Make questions.

1 you and your friends / look at / the new social networking site?
Are you and your friends going to look at the new social networking site?
2 your dad / use / IM?
3 teacher / buy / an interactive whiteboard?
4 you / read / a blog?
5 your mom / replace / her old cell phone with a smart phone?
6 you / watch / a movie on a big screen?

Pronunciation Weak form of *to*

5a Listen to the word *to* in these questions.
3.32
1 Are you going to play on this new game console?
2 Is your dad going to buy a netbook?
3 Is your mom going to ask about broadband?
4 Are you going to listen to this digital radio?

b Listen again and repeat.
3.32

6 In pairs, ask and answer the questions in Exercise 4.

7 What about you? In pairs, talk about three pieces of technology you're going to use this week.

I'm going to go on Facebook this evening. It's my favorite social networking site.

I'm going to write a blog on the Internet about my school.

Vocabulary • Technology phrases

1 Complete the technology phrases with these verbs. Then listen, check and repeat.
3.33

> charge   chat   download   ~~go~~   send (x2)   use (x3)   write

Word list page 111
Workbook page 112

Go **online** today—buy a ticket for the technology fair.

You can .... **Wi-Fi** to play the latest games. They're really exciting!

You can .... **the Internet** on a super fast broadband connection.

You can .... **emails** to our technology experts and ask your technology questions.

You can .... **a text** to our technology contest— the prize is a netbook!

You can .... **online** with a sports star, a pop star and an actor! Ask them a question!

You can .... **a blog** about your day—take some photos, too.

You can .... **videos, music and movies**—it's all free today!

You can learn how to .... **a** new **search engine**.

You can .... **your cell phone** with a solar-powered charger—it uses energy from the sun!

2 Choose words from Exercise 1 to complete each sentence.

1 People can send information by *email* or .... .
2 You can download .... , ... or .... from the Internet.
3 You can write a .... .
4 You can chat .... with a pop star.
5 You can use .... , a .... or the .... .
6 You charge your .... with a solar-powered charger.

3 What about you? Imagine you are at a technology fair. Choose some activities to do. Make a list. Tell the class.

Morning   *use Wi-Fi to play games, … .*
Afternoon   *download movies, … .*
Evening   *write … .*

> In the morning, I'm going to use Wi-Fi to play games.

Brain Trainer Activity 4
Go to page 120

Chatroom Asking for information

Speaking and Listening

1 Look at the photo. Where are Monica, Julia and Nick?

a at the Wildlife Club
b at a radio station
c at school

2 Listen and read the conversation. Are the statements true (T) or false (F)?
3.34

1 The Wildlife Club helped some animals last week. *F*
2 The council wanted to build a road in Willow End.
3 The club sent photos to a newspaper.
4 The council decided not to build at Willow End.
5 There are five people in the club.
6 The club isn't looking for new members.

3 Act out the conversation in groups of four.

DJ	Welcome to Radio X! I'm talking to a Wildlife Club today. Hi, guys! Now, last month your Wildlife Club helped some animals. Can you tell us more?
Julia	Yes. We found rare otters in Willow End, but the city council wanted to build a new neighborhood there.
DJ	What happened?
Nick	We took photos of the otters to the newspaper, and the council isn't building it now.
DJ	That's awesome! Now, tell me about your club.
Monica	Well, it's small—four people … and a dog!
DJ	And what are you planning?
Julia	Well, this summer we're creating a nature reserve for the otters, so we're looking for more members.
DJ	OK, we're helping the club to find more members, so call in now!
Nick	Thank you.

Say it in your language …
That's awesome!
Well, …

4 **Look back at the conversation. Who says what?**

1 Can you tell us more? *DJ*
2 What happened?
3 That's awesome!
4 Tell me about your club.
5 What are you planning?
6 Well, this summer we're creating a nature reserve.

5 **Look back at the conversation again. What phrases does the DJ use to ask about these things?**

1 the club
2 the club's plans for the summer

6 **Read the phrases for asking for information.**

Past	Present	Future
What happened?	Can you tell us more? Tell me about …	What are you planning?

7 **Listen to the conversations. Act out**
3.35 **the conversations in pairs.**

Kenji	I'm not going on vacation this summer.
May	Oh, what are you planning?
Kenji	I'm [1] seeing my friends every day.
Tom	I got a bad grade on my [2] math test.
Olivia	Why? What happened?
Tom	Oh, I didn't understand the instructions.
Zoe	I started an awesome blog last week.
Luke	Really? Tell me about it.
Zoe	Well, it's about [3] social networking sites.

8 **Work in pairs. Replace the words in purple in Exercise 7. Use these words and/or your own ideas. Act out the conversations.**

> What are you planning this summer?

> I'm traveling to the mountains.

1 writing a blog / chatting online / going to the swimming pool

2 English homework / science test / history essay

3 the Internet / downloading music / using a search engine

Grammar • Present continuous for future arrangements

Affirmative		
I	'm (am)	going to a party tonight.
You/We/They	're (are)	
He/She/It	's (is)	

Negative		
I	'm not (am not)	playing basketball tomorrow.
You/We/They	aren't (are not)	
He/She/It	isn't (is not)	

Questions and short answers		
Are	you/we/they	watching a movie tonight?
Is	he/she/it	

Yes, I am. / No, I'm not.

Yes, you/we/they are. / No, you/we/they aren't.

Yes, he/she/it is. / No, he/she/it isn't.

Grammar reference Workbook page 102

1 **Study the grammar table.**

2 **Complete the conversations with the Present continuous affirmative or negative.**

A Are *you wearing* (you / wear) dressy clothes to Oscar's party next week?
B No, …. (I / not / go) in dressy clothes.

A I …. (stay / at home) tonight. What about you? Are …. (you / go) out?
B Yes, I am. I …. (help) the Wildlife Club.

A Emma …. (not / come) to school tomorrow.
B Why not?
A Because …. (she / fly) to Los Angeles with her parents.

3 **What are these people doing this week and on the weekend?**

1 You
2 Your friend
3 You and your friends
4 Your teacher

4 **In pairs, ask and answer the questions in Exercise 3.**

> What are you doing this weekend?

> I'm going to a new dance class.

Reading

1 **Look at the text. What is it?**

a a phone conversation
b an interview
c a chatroom discussion

Technology-Free Week!

Remember, next week is the last week of the school year, and the school is having an official "technology-free" week—so the chatroom is going offline. How are YOU going to live without technology? Tell us your plans for "technology-free" week here!

Comments ▼

Why are you doing this to us? I think it's insane. In fact, it's not possible! I'm going to go crazy! I can't live without my MP3 player. It's going to be soooo difficult. I'm going to sing songs all week.
Skaterboy

Last year I went on vacation to a farm. There wasn't any TV, and we didn't have a computer. I can live without these things, but it isn't fun! I'm going to play a lot of sports next week.
Anya12

I'm going to read ... and eat. In the evenings, my friends and I are going to have parties. We're going to play music on the radio—is that OK? Is that technology?
Madmax

In my opinion, technology is a problem. We sit around all day, and we don't get much exercise. We don't talk. We can't hear because we have earphones in our ears all day. Technology-free week is a great idea! I think it's fun, too. Are you going to film us?
Smiley

Key Words		
technology-free	offline	to live without
insane	crazy	earphones

---

2 **Read and check your answer to Exercise 1.**

3 **Read the text. Are the sentences true (T) or false (F)?**
3.36

1 Skaterboy likes the idea of "technology-free" week. *F*
2 Skaterboy is going to study all week.
3 Anya12 thinks life without technology is great.
4 Anya12 is going to go to a farm.
5 Madmax is going to have a lot of parties.
6 Smiley agrees with "technology-free" week.

4 **Read the text again. Answer the questions.**
3.36

1 What is a technology-free week?
   It's a week where you can't use technology.
2 Is Skaterboy happy with the idea?
3 What is Anya12 going to do?
4 What is Madmax going to play music on?
5 Why does Smiley think that technology is a problem?

Listening

1 **Listen to the interview. Which words do you hear?**
3.37

chat	download	email	novel
online	search engine	Wi-Fi	

2 **Listen again. Answer the questions.**
3.37

1 Speaker A is going to …
   a learn to use a computer.
   b work for his dad.
   c help his grandpa.
2 Speaker B is going to …
   a go online every day.
   b teach her friends tennis.
   c go to the beach.
3 Speaker C is going to …
   a write a short story.
   b read a "keitai" novel.
   c write a Twitter novel.

Writing • A story

1 **Read the Writing File.**

> **Writing File**   Review
>
> **Remember to use all your writing skills!**
>
> **a** **Check your punctuation**
>   Do you have periods, capital letters, commas, question marks and exclamation points?
> **b** **Use linking words**
>   Use *and*, *but* or *because* to join words, phrases or sentences.
> **c** **Write in paragraphs**
>   Is the information in a group?

2 **Read the story and find more examples of each writing skill.**

The Time Machine
A short story by
Olivia da Silva, age 12

My friend, the Professor, has a Time Machine. It's amazing, but it's a secret! This evening we're going to travel to the future. I want to see my town in 2050!

The Time Machine is small and black. There's a big screen and a lot of computers. In fact, you can get Wi-Fi and download videos!

We're traveling very fast now ... BANG! What was that? We're in another time, but when?
I'm going to open the door … We're walking out into the street. People are wearing long white clothes. Oh no! We aren't in the future. We're in Rome, 2,000 years ago. It's exciting, but we're going home soon—it's late!

3 **Read the story again. Answer the questions.**

1 What is Olivia's friend's name? *the Professor*
2 Is the Time Machine big?
3 What can you do in the Time Machine?
4 Do they travel to the past?
5 How many years ago was it?
6 Why is Olivia going home?

4 **Choose the correct options to make sentences.**

1 Joanna's traveling in time , / . but I'm not.
2 Are you going to fly , / ?
3 They aren't going to the past . / ?
4 I don't have an e-reader, *and / but* my dad does.
5 William's using a search engine *but / because* he's doing his homework.
6 We're going to download music *and / but* videos this evening.

5 **Choose your means of transportation and your place. Take notes about your journey.**

Transportation time machine / space rocket
Place space / the moon / a new planet

6 **Write a story. Use "My story" and your notes from Exercise 5.**

> **My story**
>
> **Title**
> Think of a title for your story.
>
> **Paragraph 1**
> Who is your friend?
> Do you want to visit the past or the future?
> What do you want to see there?
>
> **Paragraph 2**
> Describe your time machine or space rocket.
>
> **Paragraph 3**
> Describe the place and things (and people) you can see.
>
> What place (and time) are you in?

> **Remember!**
> ● Use punctuation, linking words and paragraphs.
> ● Use the vocabulary in this unit.
> ● Check your grammar and spelling.

Refresh Your Memory!

Grammar • Review

1 **Complete the text with the correct form of *be going to*.**

We ¹ *'re going to go* (go) on vacation to Mexico this summer. We ² .... (take) a lot of things! My mom ³ .... (read) some e-books, and my dad ⁴ .... (send) emails on his smart phone in the evenings. I ⁵ .... (listen) to a lot of new songs on my MP3 player, and my two sisters ⁶ .... (do) their homework on their laptop.

2 **Make the questions for the vacation questionnaire.**

1 *Are you going to watch TV in your room?*

Vacation questionnaire

		Bella	Jessica	Freddie
1	watch TV in your room?	✗	✓	✗
2	eat pizza every week?	✓	✗	✓
3	go swimming every day?	✓	✓	✗
4	see all your friends?	✓	✓	✓
5	play basketball?	✗	✗	✓
6	do any homework?	✗	✗	✗

3 **Make six sentences about the three children in Exercise 2.**

1 *Jessica is going to watch TV in her room, but Bella and Freddie aren't going to watch TV in their rooms.*

4 **Make sentences about arrangements for tomorrow using the Present continuous.**

1 Olivia / get up / 11 a.m.
  Olivia is getting up at 11 a.m.
2 I / study / online in the morning
3 Isabella and Carlos / not go / to the movies
4 My brother / wash / Dad's car
5 Fiona / not clean up / her room
6 We / have / chicken and potatoes for dinner

Vocabulary • Review

5 **Match five technology words.**

1 *digital radio*

digital	drive	flash	instant
interactive	messaging	networking	radio
site	social	whiteboard	

6 **Choose the correct options.**

1 How often do you *use / send / go* online?
2 Can you *use / write / read* Wi-Fi at school?
3 We often *charge / use / chat* the Internet for homework.
4 Mom *uses / chats / sends* emails to all her friends at Christmas.
5 Do you *use / charge / send* many texts?
6 I often *chat / send / charge* online with my cousins in Atlanta.
7 I'm going to *read / charge / go* my cell phone before I go on vacation.
8 She doesn't often *chat / use / download* music.

Speaking • Review

7 **Match the questions (a–c) to the answers (1–3).**
3.38 **Then listen and check.**

a What are your plans for the summer?
b What happened?
c Can you tell me more?

1 I passed my exam!
2 Yes! We're doing a radio show soon.
3 I'm going to go surfing.

Dictation

8 **Listen and write in your notebook.**
3.39

 My assessment profile: Workbook page 135

Citizenship File

The Statewide Youth Council of Massachusetts

Eddie and Brianna are ordinary high school students in Massachusetts. But they also have an important job. They are members of the Statewide Youth Council. There are twenty-eight members on the Council, all between 14 and 20 years old. Their job is to represent young people in their city or town for two years.

All young people from Massachusetts can apply to be Council members, and a special committee reads their applications and chooses the best candidates. The members of the Youth Council meet every two months. They talk to the governor of Massachusetts about the problems young people face in their area. Together with the governor, they discuss their ideas and make a plan of action.

The members of the Youth Council work on many different things. For example, between 2012 and 2014, they organized an antibullying campaign in schools. They discussed bullying and possible solutions with students, and helped pass new laws against bullying. They also encouraged other young people to take part in their community. In 2015 the Youth Council is planning to focus on young people's education and health.

Eddie says, "Youth Council means that our opinion is important." Brianna adds, "But the best part is that we help make a difference in the lives of other young people."

Reading

1 Read the text quickly. Why are Eddie and Brianna important people?

2 Read the text again. Answer the questions.

3.40
1 What do Youth Council members do?
They represent young people from their city or town.

2 How many Statewide Youth Council members are there?

3 How old are the Youth Council members?

4 How long do young people work for the Youth Council?

5 What did the Youth Council do between 2012 and 2014?

My Citizenship File

3 You want to be a Youth Council member. Think about your application.

- What are the problems in your area?
- What are your ideas?

4 Write five sentences for your application in your notebook.

Grammar • Past simple: *to be*

1 **Change the sentences into the Past simple.**

1 I'm in Mexico. *I was in Mexico.*
2 He isn't a teacher.
3 Are you in the hospital?
4 Is it cold?
5 Am I late?
6 They aren't very big.

• There was/There were

2 **Complete the conversation with the correct form of *there was/there were*.**

A [1] *Was there* a party on Saturday night?
B Yes, [2] ..... It was at Sam's house.
A [3] .... a lot of people at the party?
B No, [4] ..... It was small, but it was fun!
A [5] .... any good music?
B Yes, the music was awesome. [6] .... a lot of dancing, too. Yasmin's dancing was amazing!

• Past simple

3 **Complete the sentences with the Past simple.**

1 I *stopped* (stop) at the station at 7:15 a.m.
2 He .... (study) Japanese in Tokyo for two years. Then he .... (work) for a Japanese bank.
3 I .... (call) Katie on her cell phone this morning, but she .... (not answer).
4 They .... (talk) to their mom about the problem and .... (ask) her for advice.
5 We .... (travel) around Oregon last summer, but we .... (not like) the weather!

4 **Complete the text with the Past simple form of these verbs.**

clean   cook   hate   play   rain   ~~start~~   stay   stop

The rain [1] *started* at 7 a.m. yesterday, and it [2] .... (not). It [3] .... all day. I [4] .... (not) soccer because of the weather. I [5] .... at home, and my sister and I [6] .... up our rooms. Mom [7] .... pasta for dinner, but I [8] .... the vegetables with it. Yuck! What a terrible day!

5 **What did Brandon do on Saturday? What didn't he do? Make sentences.**

1 *He got up early.*
2 *He didn't have a healthy breakfast.*

• get up early	✓
• have a healthy breakfast	✗
• go to the mall	✓
• buy a present for Cara	✗
• have lunch with Dan	✓
• do his math homework	✓
• give Cara her present	✗

6 **Complete the text with the Past simple.**

"How many seconds are there in a minute?" the teacher [1] *asked* (ask) when the students [2] .... (come) into the classroom. The question [3] .... (not be) difficult. "Sixty," they [4] .... (answer). "Good. And how many seconds in a year?" the teacher [5] .... (continue). The students [6] .... (think) for a moment, but they [7] .... (not know). Only Jim [8] .... (put) his hand up. "Twelve," he [9] .... (say). "There's January 2nd, February 2nd, March 2nd, ..."

7 **Make questions and answers with the Past simple.**

1 when / they / leave / ?   (at six thirty)
   When did they leave?
   They left at six thirty.
2 I / say / the wrong thing / ?   (yes)
3 what / he / give / his mom / ?   (a book)
4 you / understand / the question / ?   (no)
5 how many / glasses of juice / we / drink / ? (nine)
6 they / help / Matt / ?   (yes)

8 **Complete the conversation in the Past simple.**

A Where [1] *did you go* (go) on vacation this year?
B We [2] .... (travel) around Europe by train.
A Cool! How many days [3] .... (the trip, take)?
B It [4] .... (take) two weeks.
A [5] .... (you, visit) any interesting cities?
B Yes, we [6] ..... We [7] .... (see) the Eiffel Tower in Paris, and we also [8] .... (go) to Vienna, Budapest and Athens.
A [9] .... (you, come) home by train?
B No, we [10] ..... We [11] .... (fly).

• Be going to

9 Make sentences about future plans with *be going to*.

1 I / see a movie / this weekend
  I'm going to see a movie this weekend.
2 they / walk / to the park / on Saturday
3 Sally and I / not clean up / our room / tonight
4 a new store / open / in the shopping mall / soon
5 she / not come / with us / tomorrow
6 I / be / a doctor

10 Complete the conversation with the correct form of *be going to*.

A What are your plans for the weekend?
  ¹ *Are you going to be* (be) at home?
B No, I ² .... . I ³ .... (visit) my grandparents.
A ⁴ .... (your brothers, go) with you?
B Yes, they ⁵ .... .
A ⁶ .... (your mom, drive) you there?
B No, she ⁷ .... . We ⁸ .... (take) the bus.
A ⁹ .... (you, read) a book on the bus?
B Yes, I ¹⁰ .... , but my brothers ¹¹ .... (not do) that.
  They ¹² .... (play) games on their game consoles.

• Present continuous for future arrangements

11 Read this family's calendar. Make sentences about their plans.

1 *At five o'clock on Monday, Lily's playing tennis with Josh.*

Monday	Lily: 5 p.m., play tennis with Josh
Tuesday	Sam: 6 p.m., see "Tarantula" at the movie theater
Wednesday	Mom: buy food for Dad's birthday dinner Lily and Sam: cook the dinner
Thursday	Lily and Sam: do gymnastics after school
Friday	Mom and Dad: 8 p.m., have dinner at the Red Café Lily: stay at Tasha's house

Speaking • Talking about the past

1 Rewrite the sentences. Use a word or phrase from each box.

ago (x3)	last (x3)	this	yesterday

afternoon	an hour	month	morning
night	~~summer~~	three weeks	twenty minutes

It's now 8 p.m. on Saturday, June 23.

1 They planned the concert in August.
  They planned the concert last summer.
2 We heard about it in May.
3 We bought the tickets on June 2.
4 I sent her an email on Friday at 3 p.m.
5 I called her on Friday at 9 p.m.
6 The game started today at 11 a.m.
7 She arrived today at 7 p.m.
8 I saw her today at 7:40 p.m.

• Talking on the phone

2 Put the conversation in the correct order.

Debbie	Hi, Edward. Is the band going to meet tonight?	....
Bill	Hello.	.1.
Debbie	Oh, good. Thanks. See you later!	....
Bill	No, it's Bill.	....
Debbie	Hi. Is this Edward?	.2.
Edward	Bye!	....
Debbie	Oh. Hi, Bill. It's Debbie. Can I speak to Edward, please?	....
Edward	Yes, it is. At six thirty.	....
Bill	OK. Hold on. Here he is.	....

• Asking for information

3 Make questions.

1 you / me / tell / Can / more / ?
2 plans / are / What / your / ?
3 happened / What / ?

Vocabulary • Ordinal numbers, years, dates

1 **Write these dates in full.**

1 Nov. 4, 1989
   November fourth, nineteen eighty-nine
2 Jan. 31, 2007   4 Feb. 15, 1995
3 Aug. 22, 2014   5 Mar. 3, 2009

• Regular verbs

2 **Complete the sentences with the correct Past simple form of these verbs.**

answer	ask	call	~~close~~	invent	like
listen	stop	study	talk	travel	work

1 I didn't buy any food because the store *closed* early.
2 In 1885 Karl Benz .... the first car. His wife Bertha .... 100 kilometers in it in one day.
3 We .... the Romans in history last week. Jimmy .... some questions about Roman gladiators. Our teacher .... some of his questions, but she didn't know all the answers.
4 Five years ago, my dad .... at a hospital. He .... his job. He was sad when he .... working there.
5 I .... my grandma last night. We .... for a long time, and she .... to all my problems.

• Means of transportation

3 **Complete the sentences with some of these words.**

bike	boat	bus	canoe	car
helicopter	motorcycle	~~plane~~	scooter	
subway	train	truck	van	

1 Forty people are going from Madrid to Paris. They can go by *plane* or .... .
2 A family of six needs to travel three kilometers in New York City. But no one has a bike. They can go by .... or .... .
3 You are taking 200 kilos of apples to different stores in the city. You can use a .... or a .... .
4 You want to travel on water. You can use a .... or a .... .

• Clothes

4 **Put these clothes into the correct categories.**

boots	coat	dress	hat	jeans
pants	pajamas	sandals	scarf	shoes
shorts	skirt	~~sneakers~~	sweater	T-shirt

on your feet	in bed	on your legs	for cold weather	other
sneakers, ...				

• Technology

5 **Complete the words with the missing letters.**

1 I often do my homework on my n <u>e</u> t <u>b</u> <u>o</u> <u>o</u> k.
2 I like reading novels on my e-r _ _ d _ r.
3 We're listening to our d _ _ it _ _ r _ _ _ o.
4 What's on that f _ _ _ h dr_ _ _?
5 He writes an interesting b _ _ _ about his life.
6 He has b _ _ _ db _ _ d but no W _-F _.
7 We have an int _ _ ac _ _ _ _ w _ _ t _ b _ _ _ d in our classroom.
8 Your computer has a big s _ _ _ _ n!
9 She often goes on s _ c _ _ l n _ _ w _ _ k _ _ _ s _ t _ s, but she never uses i _ _ t _ _ t m _ _ s _ _ _ _ g.

6 **Complete the text with these words.**

chat	charge	~~download~~	get	go
read	send	use	write	

I love technology. I [1] *download* a lot of music and videos, and I often [2] .... search engines for my homework. My life is very boring, so I don't [3] .... a blog about it. But my sister is traveling in Asia, and I [4] .... her blog every day. My friends and I often [5] .... online after school, about teachers, homework, everything! I [6] .... my cell phone every night, so it always has power for the next day. I can't [7] .... online with it because it isn't a smart phone. But I [8] .... a lot of texts to my friends, and I [9] .... a lot of texts from them, too.

Word list

Unit 7 • Modern History

Ordinal numbers, years, dates

fifth	/fɪfθ/
first	/fɚst/
fourth	/fɔrθ/
second	/ˈsɛkənd/
third	/θɚd/
thirty-first	/ˈθɚt̬i fɚst/
twentieth	/ˈtwɛntiɪθ/
twenty-second	/ˈtwɛnti ˈsɛkənd/
nineteen fifty-seven	/ˌnaɪnˈtin ˈfɪfti ˈsɛvən/
nineteen forty-two	/ˌnaɪnˈtin ˈfɔrt̬i ˈtu/
nineteen ninety	/ˌnaɪnˈtin ˈnaɪnti/
nineteen twelve	/ˌnaɪnˈtin ˈtwɛlv/
nineteen twenty-two	/ˌnaɪnˈtin twɛnti ˈtu/
twenty eleven	/ˈtwɛnti ɪˈlɛvən/
two thousand	/ˈtu ˈθaʊzənd/
two thousand four	/ˈtu ˈθaʊzənd ənd ˈfɔr/

Regular verbs

answer	/ˈænsɚ/	answered	/ˈænsɚd/
ask	/æsk/	asked	/ˈæskt/
call	/kɔl/	called	/kɔld/
close	/kloʊz/	closed	/kloʊzd/
invent	/ɪnˈvɛnt/	invented	/ɪnˈvɛntɪd/
like	/laɪk/	liked	/ˈlaɪkt/
listen	/ˈlɪsən/	listened	/ˈlɪsənd/
stop	/stɑp/	stopped	/stɑpt/
study	/ˈstʌdi/	studied	/ˈstʌdɪd/
talk	/tɔk/	talked	/tɔkt/
travel	/ˈtrævəl/	traveled	/ˈtrævəld/
work	/wɚk/	worked	/wɚkt/

Unit 8 • Travel

Means of transportation

bike	/baɪk/
boat	/boʊt/
bus	/bʌs/
canoe	/kəˈnu/
car	/kɑr/
helicopter	/ˈhɛləˌkɑptɚ/
motorcycle	/ˈmoʊt̬ɚˌsaɪkəl/
plane	/pleɪn/
scooter	/ˈskut̬ɚ/
subway	/ˈsʌbweɪ/
train	/treɪn/
truck	/trʌk/
van	/væn/

Clothes

boots	/buts/
coat	/koʊt/
dress	/drɛs/
hat	/hæt/
jeans	/dʒinz/
pajamas	/pəˈdʒɑməz, -ˈdʒæ-/
pants	/pænts/
sandals	/ˈsændəlz/
scarf	/skɑrf/
shoes	/ʃuz/
shorts	/ʃɔrts/
skirt	/skɚt/
sneakers	/ˈsnikɚz/
sweater	/ˈswɛt̬ɚ/
T-shirt	/ˈti ʃɚt/

Unit 9 • Technology Time

Technology

blog	/blɑg/
broadband	/ˈbrɔdbænd/
digital radio	/ˈdɪdʒɪtl ˈreɪdiˌoʊ/
e-reader	/ˈiˌridɚ/
flash drive	/ˈflæʃ draɪv/
IM (instant messaging)	/aɪ emˌ ˈɪnstənt ˈmɛsɪdʒɪŋ/
interactive whiteboard	/ˌɪntəˈræktɪv ˈwaɪtbɔrd/
netbook	/ˈnɛtbʊk/
screen	/skrin/
smart phone	/ˈsmɑrt foʊn/
social networking site	/ˈsoʊʃəl ˈnɛtwɚkɪŋ saɪt/
Wi-Fi	/ˈwaɪfaɪ/

Technology phrases

charge your cell phone	/tʃɑrdʒ yɚ ˈsɛl foʊn/
chat online	/tʃæt ˌɑnˈlaɪn/
download movies	/ˌdaʊnloʊd ˈmuviz/
download music	/ˌdaʊnloʊd ˈmyuzɪk/
download videos	/ˌdaʊnloʊd ˈvɪdioʊz/
go online	/goʊ ˈɑnlaɪn/
send a text	/sɛnd ə ˈtɛkst/
send an email	/sɛnd ən ˈimeɪl/
use a search engine	/yuz ə sɚtʃ ˈɛndʒɪn/
use the Internet	/yuz ði ˈɪntɚˌnɛt/
use Wi-Fi	/yuz ˈwaɪfaɪ/
write a blog	/raɪt ə blɑg/

Brain Trainer

Find the difference

1 Look at the photo on page 14 for one minute. Now study this photo. What differences can you find?

Grammar

2 In pairs, look at the pictures. Then cover the pictures and choose A or B. Your partner reads the sentences. Correct them.

Paulo   Mike   Anya and Hans

Paulo has a magazine.
That's wrong. Mike has a magazine.

A
1 Paulo has a magazine.
2 Anya and Hans have skateboards.
3 Hans doesn't have a guitar.
4 Mike has a wallet.

B
1 Mike has a camera.
2 Hans has a watch.
3 Mike doesn't have an MP3 player.
4 Anya and Hans have backpacks.

Vocabulary

3a Complete the words. You have two minutes!

1 p _ s t e _   5 _ a l _ e t
2 _ a p _ o p   6 g _ i _ a _
3 c _ _ i c _   7 _ V _
4 _ a m e c _ n s o _ e   8 s k _ _ _ b _ _ _ d

3b Now make three more word puzzles for your partner to guess.

4 Work in pairs. Choose a numbered picture and say the adjective that matches it. Your partner finds the opposite adjective in the lettered pictures.

> 4. Easy.

> C. Difficult.

Brain Trainer

Find the difference

1. Look at the photo on page 24 for one minute. Now study this photo. What differences can you find?

Grammar

2. Make true statements about your town or city using all the sentence beginnings below. Write the sentences in your notebook. You have two minutes!

In my town/city, there are ... .

There's a ... .

There isn't a ... .

There are (two) ... .

There aren't any ... .

There are some ... .

Vocabulary

3a. How many places in a town can you remember that have the letter *a* in them? Think of ten.

1 *hospital*

3b. Label the places in the pictures.

a *hospital*

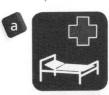

4. Work in pairs. Choose six words from the list. Tell your partner what to do. Then switch roles.

bike	climb	dance	fly
juggle	jump	play	run
sing	skate	swim	walk

Walk (please) ... .
(Now) jump ... .

Brain Trainer

Find the difference

1 Look at the photo on page 34 for one minute. Now study this photo. What differences can you find?

Grammar

2 Make five sentences using all the words from the orange, purple and blue boxes.

1 *I get up at 7 a.m.*

I	She	Sam	You	They

do homework	like	get up
goes to the movies	doesn't like	

math	after school	on Fridays
pizza	at 7 a.m.	

Vocabulary

3a Read the phrases in the box aloud three times. Cover the box. Read the list below. Which phrase is missing?

> get up → take a shower → get dressed → have breakfast → start school → have lunch

get up → take a shower → have breakfast → start school → have lunch

3b Now try again.

> go home → do homework → meet friends → have dinner → watch TV → go to bed

go home → do homework → meet friends → have dinner → go to bed

4a Look at the books. What are the subjects?

1 *art*

4b Think of four subjects that are not in the pictures.

Brain Trainer

Find the difference

1 Look at the photo on page 48 for one minute. Now study this photo. What differences can you find?

Grammar

2 Add the correct *Wh* word to make questions. You have one minute!

1 *When* do you finish school?
2 .... is my guitar?
3 .... often do you go shopping?
4 .... is your favorite writer?
5 .... do you do after school?
6 .... do you have a camera today?

3 Make sentences with words of the same color. Then make your own color puzzle. In pairs, complete your partner's puzzle.

1 *I sometimes listen to music.*

I	soccer	usually	7 a.m.	She
to	sometimes	on	often	We
I	bikes	always	never	listen
Saturday	at	to	school	get up
He	watches	play	music	TV

Vocabulary

4a Complete the crossword.

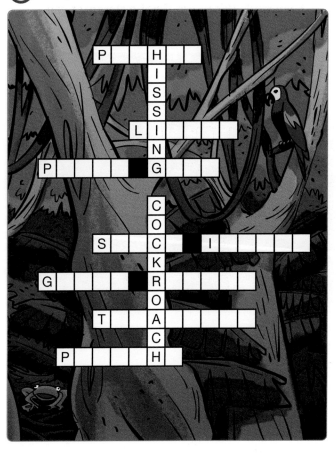

4b Two animals are missing from the puzzle. Can you name them?

5 Unscramble the words to complete the sentences with parts of the body. You have three minutes!

1 Parrots have **keabs** and **singw**.
   beaks and wings
2 Our cat has four big **waps** and a long **lait**.
3 We have ten **nerfsig** and **sote**.
4 My spider doesn't have **mars**, but it has eight **gels**.
5 Deer have small **hades** and long **skenc**.
6 Snakes don't have **teef** or **sahnd**. Sea snakes have **nifs**.

Brain Trainer

Find the difference

1. Look at the photo on page 58 for one minute. Now study this photo. What differences can you find?

Grammar

2. Look at the picture for two minutes. Cover the picture. Now say a square. Your partner says what the person is doing.

   1a – He's climbing.

Vocabulary

3. Look at the picture and find eight activities. You have two minutes!

4. Read the words in each box aloud three times. Cover the words and write them in your notebook. Can you remember all the words?

hot
sunny

warm
cloudy
windy

cold
foggy
raining
snowing

Brain Trainer

Find the difference

1. Look at the photo on page 68 for one minute. Now study this photo. What differences can you find?

Grammar

2. Work in pairs. Take turns asking questions and giving answers.

1 *How many* bananas do you have? four
2 .... pasta do we have? a lot
3 .... eggs do you have? (not) any
4 .... juice do you have? (not) much
5 .... cheese do we have? some
6 .... ham sandwiches do you have? two
7 .... tomatoes do you have? a lot
8 .... bread do we have? (not) much

How much juice do you have?

I don't have much juice.

Vocabulary

3. How many food words can you make using these letters? You have three minutes!

banana, ...

4. Put the letters in the correct order to make adjectives. You have two minutes!

1 *clean*

1 l e c n a
2 t h o
3 e l r g a
4 d c l o
5 c u s i o i d e l
6 y s n o i
7 t q u e i
8 i n g d i s u g s t
9 d r i y t
10 l l s a m
11 b h o i r r e l
12 f u l e r d n o w

Brain Trainer 7

Find the difference

1. Look at the photo on page 82 for one minute. Now study this photo. What differences can you find?

Grammar

2. Make sentences with words of the same color. Then make your own color puzzle. In pairs, complete your partner's puzzle.

1 *She was at the hospital this morning.*

She	any	morning	classroom	at
the	was	the	station	computers
weren't	wasn't	friends	the	hospital
the	I	There	were	brother
ago	in	Lucy's	My	café
fifteen	at	on	in	They
at	the	this	last	minutes
was	were	ago	TV	the
train	an	week	hour	library

Vocabulary

3a. Work in pairs. Choose list A or B. Your partner says the dates. Write them down in your notebook. Switch roles. Then check your answers.

A	B
1904	1931
1956	1989
2008	2003
2014	2012

3b. Now try again.

A	B
5/17/1833	12/1/1899
1/29/1990	2/7/1954
4/10/2000	10/20/2007
6/6/2015	8/31/2020

4a. Read the words in the box for one minute. Cover the words and write them in your notebook. How many can you remember?

asked liked talked
closed called worked

4b. Now try again.

listened studied
answered
invented stopped traveled

Brain Trainer

Find the difference

1 Look at the photos on page 92 for one minute. Now study these photos. What differences can you find?

Grammar

2 Make sentences with words of the same color. Then make your own color puzzle. In pairs, complete your partner's puzzle.

1 *I went to London yesterday.*

I	took	a	dinner	yesterday
didn't	bought	went	I	new
to	I	a	I	had
the	London	yesterday	sweater	drink
for	buy	train	pizza	I

3 Work in small groups. Act out something you did last weekend. Your classmates guess what you did. The person who gives the correct answer acts out the next activity.

 Did you play soccer?

 No, I didn't.

Vocabulary

4a Find two transportation words hidden in the grid.

m	o	t	o
c	a	r	r
r	u	l	c
e	l	c	y

4b Now make your own grid. Can your partner find the words?

5a Look at the pictures. What are these items? You have three minutes!

1 *T-shirt*

5b Can you think of five more clothes words? You wear them on your head or your feet.

Brain Trainer

Find the difference

1 Look at the photo on page 102 for one minute. Now study this photo. What differences can you find?

Grammar

2 Look at the picture for two minutes, then cover it. Now say a square. Your partner says what the people are or aren't going to do tomorrow.

3a – They aren't going to visit the museum tomorrow.

Vocabulary

3 Match ten technology words.

1 *interactive whiteboard*

flash
~~whiteboard~~
messaging
band
drive
net
broad
phone
smart
digital
e-
book
social
networking
instant
radio
reader
site
Wi-
Fi
~~interactive~~

4 Look at the pictures. What are the mystery phrases?

1 *send an email*

 an

 your

 music

4 use the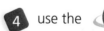

 a

 online

 a

Reading

1 Read the texts. Match the fact files (A–D) to the
3.41 correct state or city (1–4). Then listen and check.

2 Read the texts again. Answer the questions.
3.41
1 What language do most people speak
in the US?
2 Where are the following cities?
a New York City   c Washington, DC
b Los Angeles   d Chicago

Your culture

3 In pairs, answer the questions.
1 How many official languages are there
in your country?
2 What are the main ethnic groups?
3 Write a fact file for your country.
Include this information:
- location   • main cities
- population   • languages
- a fun fact about your region, city or town

The United States: Facts and Figures

The United States is made up of fifty
states. The federal government of the
US is in Washington, DC. The president
is the head of the executive branch of
the government. The other two branches
are Congress and the Supreme Court.
The United States is a multicultural
society. There is no official language,
but the vast majority of the people speak
English. There are many different ethnic
groups. People from all over the world live
in the US.

A

Location:	.... is in the midwest of the US.
Area:	149,998 km²
Population:	12.8 million
Capital:	Springfield
Main city:	Chicago
Fun fact:	The world's first skyscraper was built in Chicago in 1885.

B

Location:	.... is in the west of the US.
Area:	423,970 km²
Population:	38.8 million
Capital:	Sacramento
Main cities:	Los Angeles, San Diego, San Jose, San Francisco
Fun fact:	Frisbee, Barbie dolls and skateboards all come from this state.

C

Location:	...., is in the east of the US, between the states of Maryland and Virginia. It's the capital of the United States, and it has the status of a federal district.
Area:	177 km²
Population:	0.6 million
Fun fact:	Washington, DC, is the only city in the US that has a Spy Museum. It's a great place for James Bond fans!

D

Location:	.... is in the northeast of the US.
Area:	141,300 km²
Population:	19.7 million
Capital:	Albany
Main city:	New York City
Fun fact:	The first pizza place in the US opened in 1895 in New York City. Today some people say that New York pizza is the best pizza in the world!

Reading

1 **Read the text. Answer the questions.**

3.42

1 What are the three main stages of education in the US?
2 How many weeks of summer vacation do American students usually have?
3 Which exams do students take if they want to go to college?

2 **Read the text again. Are these statements true (T) or false (F)?**

3.42

1 Children go to elementary school from 6 to 11 years old.
2 The school year ends in August.
3 Students have lunch at school.
4 Education isn't free for children in the US.
5 American students wear a uniform in public schools.

Your culture

3 **In pairs, answer the questions.**

1 What are the main stages of education in your country?
2 Write a list of the main differences between your school and an American school. Think about uniforms, technology, vacations, subjects, school start and end times, exams and some interesting facts.

Education stages

Name of school stage	Age
Elementary school	5–11 years old
Middle school	11–14 years old
High school	14–18 years old

The school year

The school year begins in late August or early September and ends in May or June. The main vacations are two weeks at Christmas, one or two weeks in spring and eight to twelve weeks in summer.

Interesting facts

- Education in the US is free for children 5 to 18 years old.
- In American public schools, most students do not wear a uniform, but students in some private schools wear them.
- Students call their teachers by their last name— for example, Mr. Brown or Ms. Jones.
- Most children go to public schools, but 10% go to private schools, and 3% are home-schooled.
- Students take standardized tests every year.
- In 11th grade, students take SAT or ACT exams for college admission.

The school day

School usually starts at 8:30 or 9 a.m., and it gets out at 3 or 3:30 p.m. Students have lunch at school. They have their own "bag lunch" or a cooked school lunch. In elementary and middle school, students often have recess after lunch— free time to play outside or in the school gym.

Reading

1 Read the text quickly. Match the photos (A–D)
3.43 to each paragraph (1–4).

2 Read the text again. Answer the questions.
3.43
1 What do Americans eat for lunch?
2 Which meal do families usually
   have together?
3 What kind of food is popular at Thanksgiving?
4 Describe a typical Sunday breakfast in the US.
5 When do people usually eat gingerbread?

Your culture

3 In pairs, answer the questions.

1 Do people have special meals on holidays
  in your country? What do people cook
  for holiday meals?
2 Describe a typical breakfast in your country.
  Do people have a different breakfast
  on the weekend?
3 When do people have their lunch in your
  country? Is it a big meal, or do they have
  a bag lunch?

---

1 Breakfast

People often have a quick breakfast of cereal,
milk, fruit and juice during the week.
On the weekends, people have eggs, bacon,
sausage, potatoes, toast and pancakes or
waffles for breakfast.

2 American lunch

People often have cold ham and cheese or
turkey sandwiches for lunch with potato chips
or fruit. Some Americans have fast food for
lunch, like hamburgers and French fries.

3 Dinner

Dinner is the traditional time for families
to eat together. They cook a main dish
like beef, pork or chicken and eat it with
potatoes or vegetables. Many people also have
Mexican, Italian or Chinese food for dinner.

4 Holiday meals

Most families have their Thanksgiving
or Christmas meals in the late afternoon.
At Thanksgiving, people usually have roast
turkey with cranberry sauce and pumpkin pie.
A typical Christmas dinner usually includes
roast beef, ham or goose, mashed potatoes,
fruitcake and gingerbread.

Meal times

In the US, the main meal times are:

Breakfast	7–9 a.m.
Lunch	12–2 p.m.
Dinner	6:30–8 p.m.

Dinner is usually the main meal of the day.

Reading

1 **Read the text quickly and look at the photos.**
3.44 **Match the headings (1–5) to each paragraph (A–E).**

1 Water transportation
2 Taxis
3 Biking and walking
4 Buses
5 Subway

2 **Read the text again. Answer the questions.**
3.44
1 Why do a lot of people use public transportation in New York?
2 How many subway stations are there?
3 What two things can you see from the Staten Island Ferry?
4 How many people travel by bike every day?
5 What do you use to pay your fare on a bus?
6 What color are New York City cabs?

Your culture

3 **In pairs, answer the questions.**

1 What are the main means of transportation in your major cities?
2 How do students get to your school?
3 Write a short paragraph to describe one of the means of transportation in your capital city.

New York

is a very populous city, and there are a lot of ways to travel around it. Traveling by car is expensive and often slow because of traffic, so many people use public transportation.

A ...
There are 468 subway stations and 24 different lines. New York has one of the largest subway systems in the world.

B ...
Manhattan is an island. Over 19 million people a year take the Staten Island Ferry. Some take it to go to work, and other passengers are tourists. From the boat, you can see the Statue of Liberty and the lower Manhattan skyline.

C ...
Over 200,000 city residents travel by bike every day. In fact, biking and walking together make up 21% of all trips in New York City.

D ...
More than 2 million people travel on the New York City buses every day. Over 5,900 buses run on over 200 local and express routes in the city. Passengers on a bus can use the same fare card that they use on the subway. There are also special yellow buses that take New York children to school.

E ...
New York City taxis, or cabs, are known for their distinctive yellow color. Over 13,000 taxis operate in the city. The taxi drivers know every street in New York City. It's a very hard job!

Reading

1 Read the text quickly. Complete each paragraph
3.45 with the correct information.

  a Rock'n'Roll
  b swim fins and eyeglasses
  c about 1,800 poems
  d Civil Rights Movement

2 Read the text again. Are these statements
3.45 true (T) or false (F)?

  1 The United States declared independence
    from France.
  2 Emily Dickinson published her poems
    in magazines.
  3 Elvis is often called the Prince.
  4 Martin Luther King Jr. was a leader of
    the African-American community.

Your culture

3 In pairs, do these activities.

  1 Write the names of five famous people from
    your country and say why they are famous.
    • a writer
    • a sports star
    • a painter
    • an actor
    • a scientist
  2 Write a short paragraph about one
    of the famous people from your country.
    Include this information:
    • Date of birth
    • Where does (did) he/she live?
    • What does (did) he/she do?
    • Why is (was) he/she famous?

■ Benjamin Franklin (1706–1790)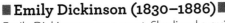

Benjamin Franklin is best known as one of the politicians
who signed the American Declaration of Independence
from Great Britain. However, he was also an author,
a printer, a scientist, a diplomat and an inventor. We still
use some of Franklin's inventions, such as [1] ..... .

■ Emily Dickinson (1830–1886)

Emily Dickinson was a poet. She lived a quiet and private
life, and she never got married or had children. She wrote
[2] ...., but she only shared some of them with her family
and friends. When Dickinson died, her family decided to
publish her poetry. Now Emily Dickinson is considered one
of the greatest American poets.

■ Elvis Presley (1935–1977)

Elvis Presley was an American singer and actor.
He is often called the King of [3] ...., or simply the King.
He sold 600 million of his albums around the world.
He died almost 40 years ago, but his music still inspires
artists today.

■ Martin Luther King Jr. (1929–1968)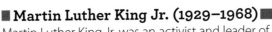

Martin Luther King Jr. was an activist and leader of the
African-American [4] ..... . He organized peaceful protests
and demonstrations against racism and discrimination
directed at African Americans. In 1964 he received the
Nobel Peace Prize for his work. Four years later, he was
assassinated in Memphis, Tennessee.

Culture American Festivals and Holidays

Reading

1 Read the text quickly and match the photos (A–D) to each festival or holiday.
3.46

2 Read the text again. Answer the questions.
3.46
1 What do people give each other on Valentine's Day?
2 What happens in some cities and towns on the Fourth of July?
3 Why do American children enjoy Halloween?
4 Who do Americans remember on Thanksgiving?

Your culture

3 In pairs, do these activities.
1 Write a list of festivals and celebrations from your country.
2 Describe a special festival or celebration. Include this information:
• When is it?
• Where is it?
• Do you eat special food?
• How do you celebrate it?

Valentine's Day

Valentine's Day falls on February 14. It's a popular holiday in the US, celebrating love and friendship. People give each other cards and small gifts, such as chocolates, flowers or teddy bears, to show their love, friendship or respect. Some people also organize Valentine's Day parties or dinners with their friends or family.

Independence Day

This public holiday is also known as the Fourth of July. It celebrates the day the United States adopted the Declaration of Independence. Some cities and towns organize Fourth of July parades and fireworks displays. Many people also spend this holiday with their families and have a barbecue or a picnic.

Halloween

Halloween is celebrated on October 31. It's a popular holiday among children, who put on scary or funny costumes and visit their neighbors, asking them for candy. Teenagers and adults sometimes wear costumes too, but they usually celebrate Halloween by going to parties or by watching scary movies.

Thanksgiving

Thanksgiving falls on the fourth Thursday of November. On that day, Americans remember the early settlers—the Pilgrims—who held a big celebration to thank God for a good harvest. Most families have a special dinner and serve some of the foods that the Pilgrims had at their feast. The most popular Thanksgiving dishes are roast turkey with cranberry sauce and sweet potatoes, along with cornbread and pumpkin pie.